essentials

Drawing Companion

essentials

Drawing Companion

Viv Foster

Oceana

AN OCEANA BOOK

This book is produced by
Oceana Books
6 Blundell Street
London
N7 9BH

Copyright © 2006 Quantum Publishing Ltd

This edition printed 2006

ISBN-10: 0-681-45880-1
ISBN-13: 978-0-681-45880-2

QUMED22

Manufactured in Hong Kong by
Modern Age Repro House Ltd
Printed in China by
CT Printing Ltd

Contents

Introduction to drawing

PEN AND INK

by Judy Martin

Man has always felt the need to represent everything that he sees, and he found that drawing was the most interesting means to carry out this desire. The first drawings can be traced back to around 35,000 years ago, when Homo sapiens scratched pictures with the sharpened-stone tool onto the walls of his cave dwelling. These cave drawings represented events in daily life such as the planting of crops or their hunting victories. Fine examples of these primitive forms of drawing can be found in the cave paintings of Altamira, in Cantabria, Spain.

The ability of a simple symbol to represent a complex notion, or even a story, makes images an essential means of communicating ideas. The style and craftsmanship of the artist combine with the drawn image to strengthen the message it puts across.

Drawing can be many different things; it is possible to stretch the definitions to cover anything from a finely-worked objective study of the world-as-seen to an idea with a line around

A drawing which concentrates on line can still make a feature of color. This pen and ink drawing picks up the cues of local color in green and red variegated plants. The drawing technique allows a clear expression of the naturally interesting composition of the plant group.

This urban landscape of trees seen through park gates is drawn in waxed-based colored pencils. Again, great subtlety of color is achieved by the overlaying of one color on top of another, giving a richness similar to oil pastels.

it! Throughout history, the master draftsmen have provided us with copious examples of the variety and scope that can be achieved by this method of making pictures.

One way of attempting to define this many-sided subject is of recording what it cannot be. It cannot be listless, for instance; a sense of investigative urgency is the basis of good drawing and listlessness is its antithesis. While it can be bold, free, generous, and full, it cannot be undisciplined, for this means that the medium controls the image beyond the accept-able bounds of experimentation and new discovery. It can be colored, but it cannot be painted in the sense that a finished watercolor can be. The definitions, then, do find their frontiers, but between these poles feel free to discover, as did so many of the great innovative draftsmen of the past, your own language—and make sure it contains many dialects.

Drawing is an activity that can be carried on almost anywhere. No specialist equipment is required; a few simple tools are all that are

NATURAL FLOWERS
by Jan McKenzie

The artist has made an interesting contrast between a sheaf of subtly colored natural flowers and the patterned paper in which they are wrapped. The printed pattern is delineated using white line technique.

needed. Size, too, is a consideration that makes the medium particularly appealing. A drawing can be as large or as small as the artist desires; some of the most striking results are achieved on a small scale. The classic example is the pocket sketch book; this is easy to carry around and, as an important extra, usually contains sufficient variety of surfaces to allow for the rendering of different visual notes.

As well as such practical considerations, however, there is no doubt that drawing has a deep psychological appeal. Children, for instance, draw before they can even walk or talk, while artists throughout history have delighted in the medium. Its essence lies in the actual physical action—the mark of the chosen tool on the paper or other support. This is the case whether the results are, say, fluid and calligraphic, or dramatic and even violent.

STUDY OF FRUITS
by Jan McKenzie

Oil pastel and colored pencils are combined in this series of fruit drawings. The artist has created a lively variation in the direction and texture of the marks. The density of color is built up by using cross-hatching with the colored pencils and stippling with pastels.

There are, of course, other factors to be taken into consideration. In particular, what might be called the artistic intention of the line and the character of the medium being used combined to give the drawing character, force, and authority. Traditionally, this has been an integral part of Oriental art; in more recent times, many Western artists have demonstrated it as well.

It is often a great surprise the first time to discover the range of images and techniques to be found in the art of drawing. The dictionary definition is far too narrow to be of any real value in understanding the breadth of work that an art

THE SINGLE DOORWAY
by David Ferry

The artist composed this picture from a series of photographs that he reproduced in a collage form using colored pencils and artist's colored inks.

PASTEL STUDY
by Moira Clinch

The quality of color and intense light in this pastel drawing, comes both from the high-key, restricted color range and from careful positioning of the highlights.

historian would include in the category of drawn images. However, many people still think that drawing is carried out only with a pencil and it consists mainly of outlines. This book aims to disprove this theory, and hopefully will give you the enthusiasm to start drawing with a number of different techniques and media.

Until relatively recently, it was unusual for drawings to be produced for purely aesthetic purposes. Because they were used as a means of study, such as Leonardo da Vinci's drawings were, or as preliminary sketches to be developed further in paintings or sculpture, drawings were regarded as a secondary medium in relation to the painted or finished work. It was not really until the mid-eighteenth century that drawing became an art form in its own right.

MEDIA

The materials you need for drawing are not many, but they need to be of a high quality if your drawing is to last. A work of art may be judged and appreciated on may levels—its qualities are numerous but the quality of the technique and style of the artist, while being of foremost importance, are nonetheless tempered by the quality of the materials used. It is the physical ingredients in a work of art that add life and beauty to the image and it is these "ingredients" that can easily determine both your end result and the way in which you work.

Pencil and graphite

Pencils offer the most direct, and the most versatile, means of allowing our thoughts to flow from the mind through the finger tips to a sheet of paper. The artist is concerned with varying degrees of softness to express different qualities in a drawing. There is usually a choice of twelve grades, from the pale, hard lines of a 6H to the soft, graduated tones of 6B. Most artists tend to work with a medium-soft pencil—grade 2B or 3B—and these can render most of the tones required. Harder pencils are sometimes useful when trying to render structure or architectural subjects. The quality of line and tone will depend to some extent on the choice of paper used.

Pencil covers a wider range of medium than is commonly thought. The lead pencil is now quite an uncommon medium, although still available. The lead pencil's light, silvery, gray line can produce an effect not dissimilar to that of silverpoint, which, before the innovation of the modern graphite pencil, was the main linear drawing instrument, particularly among Renaissance artists, although that too is in less common use today.

The graphite pencil as we know it today is often incorrectly called a "lead pencil." It is a relatively new drawing instrument and has been in common use for only about 200 years. It comes in a variety of grades. The softest grades are denoted by the letter B and range from B to 8B, which is the softest. F, HB, and H are in the middle of the range. H pencils are the hard range, from 2H to 8H. There are other grading systems but the H and B system is the most common. If in doubt, always test pencils before you buy them. The solid graphite stick, normally graded approximately at 3B, is also very useful for larger, tonal, pencil drawings, and is often used in conjunction with a regular pencil.

A pencil can be used in a variety of ways but is most commonly employed in making a line; the result is a crisp, clear drawing. Shadow can be produced by hatching or cross-hatching, which is a set of parallel lines or two opposing sets of parallel lines, respectively. The softer variety of pencil can produce very soft areas of tone using the finger or torchon, or by spreading with an eraser. The flexibility of the pencil allows for a great amount of variation and experimentation.

TERRACED HOUSES

Pencil is an excellent medium for drawings in which the artist wishes to include all the complex details of a densely textured subject. A 2B or 3B pencil can be given a fine point for linear detail, but is also soft enough to provide a good range of tones.

YOUNG CHILD

This delightful pencil study captures the round softness of the child's face. The form of the cheek has been further enhanced by lighting the subject from the top right hand corner, and the soft suggestion of shadow under the cheek, gives that part of the face a fullness you would expect in such a young child.

Colored pencils

Colored pencils come in many varieties, all made in roughly the same way, but their qualities vary from manufacturer to manufacturer and from range to range. The shape and texture of colored pencils—thin sticks of bound pigments encased in wood—provide a finer and more essentially linear drawing quality than pastels or crayons. Different types vary in the texture of the colored "lead." Some have hard, relatively brittle leads, that can be shaped into long, sharp points for very precise line work, while others are naturally soft and crumbly, more manageable than pastels but characteristically producing a broader, more grainy line than the hard pencils. The differences are caused by the binding agent used to hold the pigments. You can see and feel differences of texture if you look closely at the range of colored pencils in a display stand, but you will only know the precise drawing quality when you start to work with them.

Colored pencils characteristically produce a translucent effect that allows you to layer color marks to produce mixed hues and tones. Individual ranges may provide more than 60 colors. You can choose whether to maintain the same textural quality by using a single type in a drawing, or to take advantage of the range of textures by mixing different brands. You will probably need to use fixative to stabilize the

LANDSCAPE
by Moira Clinch

In this landscape drawing Moira Clinch shows how soft colored pencils have been used to create layered marks woven into mixed hues and tones. Working the pencil marks in one direction, in this case vertically, gives the overall image a cohesive surface.

drawing surface, either while the work is in progress of when the drawing is completed, especially if you use the softer types.

Some manufacturers produce water-soluble colored pencils that can be used either dry or wet. When you have laid the color on paper, it can be spread using a soft brush wetted with clean water. This enables you to produce effects of line and wash with the single medium. You can also dip the pencil point in water and twist and turn it on the paper to make vivid calligraphic marks.

However you choose your pencils it is a good idea to buy a few of each range available and

practice with them for a while. You will most probably want to use more than one range and may well end up buying a couple of small sets of dry colors and a small set of water-soluble pencils. Sets are often the best point at which to start because they offer a predetermined color range and capability and can be easily expanded in areas where you find the need for a greater range of pigments. Most manufacturers sell sets in numbers of 6, 12, 18, 24, and so on. A range of 12 or 18 is the ideal point at which to start because it will force you to experiment with color mixing rather than relying on pure, manufactured pigments.

Pen and ink

Pen and ink is not a medium for the faint-hearted: decision-making takes place before committing pen to paper and mistakes are difficult to erase. The quality of line is critical to the success of the drawing. That is why the traditional nib is so much better than a mechanical drawing pen, which offers no variety in the thickness of line. The pen drawings of Van Gogh, for instance, make use of the characteristic strokes of both nib and pen, with thick and thin lines used with uneven pressure. Segonzac is another artist whose work demonstrates an exquisite feeling for line.

Dip pens are inexpensive and can hold a variety of nibs from fine to broad chisel-edged shapes (*see below*). Brass reservoirs can be attached to some nibs to retain more ink, but they tend to clog easily and need cleaning frequently. Fountain pens work best with non-waterproof ink, though some pens are made specifically to be used with waterproof drawing implements, such as the traditional quill (that can be made from pigeon feathers) or sharpened bamboo. The quality of line produced is quite different from that made by a metal nib. There are a number of dense, black drawing inks available.

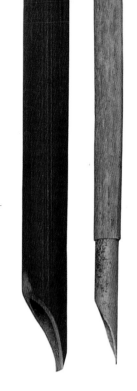

BAMBOO QUILLS

Bamboo pens and quills have very long histories, but are still made today.

ANEMONES

A colorful image can be achieved using only line work and a limited color range, as in this pen and ink drawing of anemones.

PEN AND INK LINE DRAWING

This type of drawing usually illustrates a builder's or architect's brochure. The aim of the drawing is to concentrate the viewer's mind on the building that is for sale.

The effects that can be achieved with an ink-loaded brush are numerous. Broad washes of dilute ink can be contrasted with fine but strong lines of more concentrated color. Crosshatching, stippling, splattering, and the sharp freely drawn line can all be used. Drawings can be given a softly graded tonality or high contrast depending on the visual requirements of the artist.

Drawing in colored inks, both with a limited and a comprehensive range of colors, can stretch the possibilities of pen and ink drawing further. These inks add dimension, not only as washes of color, but also when used to describe objects in their identifiable local colors. Pens and nibs can be varied and a wide range of colored inks used, perhaps consolidating the tones by the addition of a stronger, neutral ink. Tones can present a problem, it being imperative that all colors conform to an overall tonal scheme within the piece. A well resolved monochromatic drawing might prove the best foundation for color, used either as the juxtaposition of lines in various colors to effect an optical color mix or as single colors to describe objects.

Charcoal

AVOCET WADING
by Stephen Paul Plant

Charcoal can be a surprisingly delicate medium, combining well with pastel and useful both for defining details and building up dark, rich colors.

Charcoal has many advantages for the beginner. Large areas of tone can be put in very rapidly, and the intensity can be altered by various methods.

Because charcoal is a broader medium than pencil it prevents over-elaboration of unnecessary detail. It is, however, both sensitive and flexible, and can be used lightly to produce delicate, spidery lines or with greater pressure to render dark, intense shadow areas. It can also be smudged to soften a line or tone, or lifted out with a putty eraser either to create highlights or correct mistakes. Charcoal comes in many different forms, so select one that will be most suited to your needs. Charcoal pencils or thin sticks of will charcoal are generally best for linear work, while the thicker sticks are more suitable for tonal studies.

Blending techniques allow you to suggest a range of different textures. For instance, for a highly reflective material such as satin you can create subtle gradations of tone by rubbing the charcoal with a torchon or rag, working back into the drawing to define edges of folds if necessary,

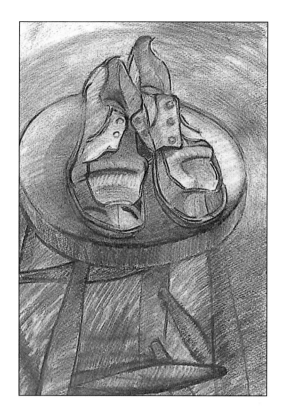

WORN PAIR OF SHOES

This charcoal drawing of a well worn pair of shoes on a stool has been rendered in a way to give a sense of the character, not only of the shoes, but also of the wearer.

YOUNG SAPLINGS

It might not be immediately apparent that this drawing was rendered in compressed charcoal. The artist has made advantage of the uniformly dense quality that compressed charcoal can give.

and using an eraser to make the highlights. A putty eraser allows you to create positive, precisely shaped white areas, and can also be used with the minimum pressure to modify tones.

For the duller surfaces of materials such as wool, a slight rubbing is usually sufficient for the highlights, which are relatively unobtrusive, and a compressed charcoal can be brought in for the more intense shadow areas.

If you are going to use erasing methods extensively it is wise to experiment a little beforehand with the paper. Generally a hard paper with a slight tooth is best as this will give depth to the charcoal and also allow the drawing to be erased without too much damage to the surface of the paper.

Pastels

Soft pastels are a source of clear, brilliant color. the quality of the pigment is very little affected by the small amount of binding medium used to contain the powdery color in stick form. Though individual pastel strokes lay down clean, opaque color, the gradual build-up of powder on the drawing surface can create a muddy, veiled effect. This cannot be eliminated altogether, but experience in handling pastels teaches you how to maintain the color values or rework them to retrieve their clarity. Fixatives, which set the loose color in place, help to control surface effect in work in progress, as well as protecting the finished drawing, and a good-quality fixative should not cause any change in the drawing's color and textures.

Medium and hard pastels contain more binding medium than soft ones, and are relatively more stable, but they do also develop a film of loose color and remain liable to smudging. When you work with pastel your fingers quickly become coated with color, and for this reason some types of pastel are paper-cased, and others protected with a fine plasticized coating for easier handling. Pastel pencils, in which the thin sticks of color are encased in wood, are cleaner to handle, but less versatile. You cannot use them to lay in broad areas of color, as you can by using the side of the pastel stick, nor can you make the particular sharp

STORMY
by Judy Martin

The strange hard light that sometimes precedes a storm is conveyed by the sharp contrast of bright orange against gray–blue in this pastel and gouache drawing.

PASTEL STROKES

The clarity or density of soft pastel color depends on the closeness of the marks and the edge quality of the pastel stick, varying from sharp lines to solid, grainy color.

line quality that the section edge of a round or square pastel stick creates.

High-quality artists' pastels are produced in tints (pale tones) and shades (dark tones) of a wide range of pure hues to facilitate tonal gradations and color blends. Boxed pastel sets offer selected colors, some representing a "basic" palette for color mixing and others representing color families—a range of reds or greens or a particular combination of colors such as greens, blues, and browns for rendering landscape.

OIL PASTELS The binding agent—a mixture of wax and fat—in oil pastels gives the color sticks a greasy texture. Broadly speaking, this is a cruder medium than soft pastels, and the color range is relatively limited. Oil pastels do not crumble into powder, so they are in some respects easier to control, but they can produce an unpleasantly smeared effect if handled carelessly. A thick application of oil pastel produces a solid layer of color that can be used to draw "negatively," by scraping back the color.

MEN IN WHITE
by Sally Strand

The network of vibrant color in the shadows, with purples, blues, and yellows woven together on the warm yellow-brown of the paper, demonstrates the artist's exceptional skill with pastels.

EXPERT TIP
Powder color—with soft pastels, you can scrape the edge of the stick with a knife or scissor-blade to release the colored powder, then spread the powder on the paper using your fingers or a rag.

Water-soluble pencils

It is true to say that all colored pencils are soluble to some extent, as you may already known if you have ever licked colored pencils to obtain lovely, smooth, bright colors. But some colored pencils are deliberately manufactured to be soluble, whereas others are not intended to be used that way. Soluble pencils are marketed as water-soluble, although if you try a range of liquid solvents, from saliva to water and turpentine, a measure of liquidity will be achievable with most leads. In destroying the bonded pigment you can create a version of watercolor painting, or you can use the medium to intensify dry color, heightening and refining the more granular effect you get with most pigment.

Caran d'Ache, Venus, and Rexell all manufacture water-soluble pencils in large ranges of colors. But do experiment thoroughly before starting work because they require a much quicker method of working than dry or dampened pigments do, and mistakes are not so easily rectified. They cannot simply be rubbed out without des-

RANUNCULUS

After sketching in the position of the still life with an HB pencil, the artist used dark carmine, black, and pale geranium lake watercolor pencil, applied with small hatched strokes, to build up the color fairly heavily.

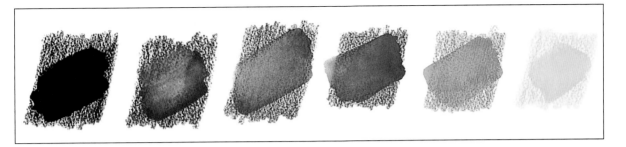

EXPERT TIP

Although blending color is one of the main attractions of this medium, it can also prove to be a problem where highlights are concerned. Either mark the "white" highlights very clearly and avoid them, mask them with masking fluid, or burnish in a white area very heavily with pencil.

THE EFFECT OF WATER ON COLOR

The swatches of color, above,. illustrate a basic palette of water-diluted colors. Notice how pale colors do not change as perceptibly as darker ones do.
The fused bands of color, below, indicate how the dissolved colors change their tones while increasing the vibrance of their hues and the subtlety of their saturation.

troying the surface of the paper, particularly if even slightly damp.

In many drawings you may wish to make a combination of water-dissolved color and dry pigment. This can be very effective when the dry color is added over a dissolved base, but remember to let the paper dry sufficiently or it will not only moisten the pencil point and produce an inky line, but it will most probably tear the paper. Also bear in mind that when you are handling liquids, they tend to spread fast. Complete blending can, of course, be achieved with water-soluble pencils but many effects, some of a very complex nature, can be created through the combination of dry and water-soluble pigments.

Experiment using both media by laying areas of tone and hatching in a variety of colors and running a complementary colored wash over the top. Try also laying dry pigment in an area and running a water-soluble color up to it. This will result in a great sense of texture that will offer increased scope for producing three-dimensional effects. Experiment with small sketches, drawing a simple object in dry, hard pigment and running behind it a background wash with a water-soluble pencil—the results are often very striking.

Markers and felt-tip pens

Markers have recently become an extremely important medium for certain types of drawing, particularly in the areas of design and graphic presentation. They are quick, convenient, and available in a wide range of coordinated colors, enabling artists to rapidly produce quite detailed and impressive color visuals that would take hours to do with paint.

The drawback, however, is the unpredictable lifespan of marker colors, as they change and fade on prolonged exposure to natural light. All artists' media are slightly variable from one pigment to another, but for practical purposes they are relatively stable, whereas some types of marker or felt-tip pen colors degrade quite quickly.

One solution is to use these media in combination with others, and to apply fixative, which

QUICK SKETCHES

Markers are excellent for quick sketches giving them a vivid impression of form and color which can later be developed through more detailed drawings. Overlaying the transparent colors creates a sense of depth and the movement of the pen tip contributes a vigorous quality to the subject even when, as above and right, it is rendered only as simple color blocks.

CALLE MARCO POLO, TANGIERS
by Paul Hogarth

This drawing demonstrates the impact of a controlled use of the bright colors that are characteristic of marker pens.

slows the degradation of color values. They are certainly extremely useful tools for sketching and working drawings, being a source of varied and fluid color that is also easily portable and does not require use of a diluent or solvent. In these contexts permanence is not essential. Keeping examples of your sketches and color roughs over a period of time also provides a way of monitoring the relative stability of the colors.

Felt-tip pens and markers may have pointed or wedge-shaped nibs, either broad or fine, and may contain water-soluble or spirit-based ink. Spirit-based inks tend to spread, "bleeding" into the paper surface beyond the passage of the nib, so you need to make allowance for this if you want to work within fairly precise shapes. When working on a sketch pad, you may also find that the colors bleed through onto the next page, but you can obtain special marker pads in which the paper is formulated to resist color bleeding.

TECHNIQUES

The fine lines made by felt-tip pens give sketches a character distinctly different from that of marker work, though the colors have similar boldness. Here hatching and shading have been used to develop an interesting variety of landscape impressions.

razor blade

pencil sharpeners

Useful equipment

FIXATIVES

Many pencil pigments require fixing once they are in place. Generally the soft colored pencils are the most prone to smudging, or leave an excess of pigment on the paper surface. However, it is wise to fix all drawings to assure a reasonable durability. Fixatives are, in effect, a lacquer. They can be bought ready to use in spray cans or bottles which are sprayed through a mouth diffuser (or you can make your own).

SHARPENERS AND BLADES

The way in which you sharpen your pencils and the implement that you use to do so will determine the type and scope of pencil marks that you will be able to create. The variety of sharpening tools available through most art shops offers you every permutation for forging your leads into shapes that you wish. They range from simple pencil sharpeners to larger desk-mounted varieties, and even electric versions. These fixed-blade sharpeners all create conical, smooth-pointed leads, but offer no flexibility in the shape

of the lead and, ultimately, the line it creates. Very soft, wood-cased pencils tend to unwrap too fast with these sharpeners and you will find that crumbly leads will be exposed too much.

Soft leads need careful handling and individual attention in sharpening—with these one of a number of knife blades will offer you greater control. Try using a scalpel or a designer's knife with a fairly short blade. You could also try out a craft knife—those with extendable calibrated blades are the best. These may be snapped off once blunt and are cheap to replace. Large knives may prove difficult to handle; many have permanent blades that, although good, will blunt more readily when constantly used on wood. They may, however, suit your purpose. it is really a question of finding a knife that you can handle with ease because you will need to be precise and delicate to achieve fine results.

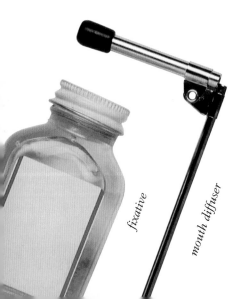

fixative

mouth diffuser

EXPERT TIPS
If you are sketching outdoors always have a good supply of fixative with you. If this is not possible, fix your drawing as soon as possible after you return home.

A finished pastel may be fixed by spraying either the front or back. From behind, the fixative permeates without dulling the color.

gum eraser

typist's eraser

ERASERS

Having applied pigment there will always be occasions when you need to remove some of it either because it was applied in error or because you want to create a particular surface effect. There are many types of erasers that you may use for this purpose and after experimenting with one or two you will probably find that having a selection on hand will be the only answer to all eventualities.

The main aim in using an eraser must be to take off pigment without disturbing the drawing surface, particularly if it is soft. Many years ago bread was used to take off color and it did little, if any, damage to the paper. Since then soft and hard erasers have been manufactured for specific use, but they cannot be used on all surfaces. Generally, hard erasers work best on hard surfaces and soft erasers on soft surfaces. Using a soft eraser on a hard surface will not offer enough key and will smudge the pigment, whereas too hard an eraser used on a soft paper will simply tear the paper.

Erasers come in many shapes and sizes. Traditional "India Rubbers" are good for general use but beware of some of the other colored varieties because they tend to leave their own pigmentation behind on your paper while removing the offending marks! The newer varieties of plastic-based erasers have soft and hard ends and offer a tighter, more solid substance to control. Plastic erasers are very useful where precise details need removing or where space is very tight because they maintain their edge and can be cut accurately with a blade to any useful shape.

Gum erasers, such as Artgum erasers are built up from excess quantities of gum. They are very malleable and offer a good soft eraser for large areas or for creating smudged or blended effects of color over wide expanses. Similar to gum erasers are kneadable erasers (or putty erasers), which can be bought from art shops. They are extremely soft and can be pressed in the hand into almost any shape.

Because of the waxy nature of colored pencil pigments it is important to keep whatever eraser you use clean—it is easy to transfer unwanted colors on a dirty eraser onto a drawing. Should it become too grubby wash the eraser in warm, soapy water. Do not, however, uses it again until it has dried thoroughly.

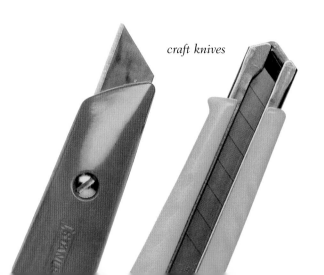

craft knives

kneadable putty eraser

scalpel

designer's knife

craft knives

Paper

PASTEL ON COLORED PAPER
by John Elliot

Pastel is traditionally associated with the use of colored grounds, allowing the line, grain, and color of the medium to achieve full vibrance. Here the dark-colored paper gives a dense, threatening mood to a wintry landscape.

Just as important a decision as the type of drawing implement you use, is your choice of paper. Paper comes in so many different compositions, surfaces, and finishes that your final choice will probably be governed by the selection available to you rather than a lack of the paper that suits your needs.

Working on white paper gives considerable versatility, as you can use opaque or transparent color, invent your own tonal range and see the interaction of marks and colors against an apparently neutral background. However, the unblemished brilliance of white paper is arguably an unnatural visual experience—there are few things that you will be able to view against a perfectly clean white ground—and there are many good reasons for including work on colored papers.

The logical reason for working on a toned or colored ground, as was the major tradition in both painting and drawing before the advent of Impressionism's pure color sensations, was to begin with a middle or neutral tone against which the lights and darks in a picture could be played at either end of the tonal scale. This method of establishing a measure for the tonal range holds good for sketching in all media, and colored paper can be less intimidating than a pure white page. However, you must remember that if you use a colored ground, you cannot get

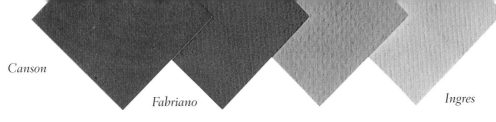

Canson

Fabriano

Canson Mi Teintes

Ingres

clear color impressions from a transparent medium such as watercolor; the underlying tone will modify both darks and lights. The idea media for this kind of work are opaque pastels and gouache, the marks from which can fully or partially conceal the ground color. It is also very useful for monochrome or limited-color drawings, when you can use, say, pencil or black crayon in contrast with a white or pale-tinted chalk or pastel, to create the extremes of tone against the central tonal or color value of your paper.

Colored papers such as the Canson Mi-Teintes, which is a light-resistant, colored-in-the-pulp drawing paper, can create beautiful effects when used with translucent colored pencils because they will alter entirely the range of colors produced. Other colored textured papers, such as Ingres, or even creamy papers like vellum, will add a new dimension to color creation as well as texture.

Consider, as well, using some of the vast ranges of machine-textured papers currently available, with effects like linen graining, elephant hide, or leather. These surfaces need not provide to be too obtrusive and, if they are used for the right purpose, will create stunning results. Think, too, about how you want to use your papers and whether you should buy pads of paper or loose sheets.

There are no real guidelines except that good papers are a joy to work with, they do not wrinkle when stretched, or scuff when rubbed under normal circumstances. They take the colored pencil pigment beautifully and are well worth the investment.

MOTHER AND CHILD
by Sally Strand

The artist has chosen blue paper to enhance the mood of her pastel subject. The gentle atmosphere is enhanced by depicting both faces in shadows against the strong summery light woven across the flesh tones and beachwear of the two figures.

Sketchbooks

FIRMLY BOUND SKETCHBOOKS

These are used a great deal by artists who build up studio paintings from sketched notes made elsewhere, especially outdoors. Such books are durable and can provide a permanent record of objects and scenes recorded over many years.

Every artist need to get into the habit of drawing frequently from observation. A sketchbook is rather like a writer's notebook; one is able to put down everyday incidents, color notes, figure studies, and ideas for composition. The sketchbook can be small enough to fit into a coat pocket, or large enough to record a fairly large landscape scene. Quite often, the artist's most interesting work will be found in his sketchbook; the small sketchbooks used by John Constable, for instance, reveal a wealth of intimate detail in terms of cloud studies, the effect of light on the landscape, and details of artefacts, such as farm wagons, all of which he used as reference for his larger paintings.

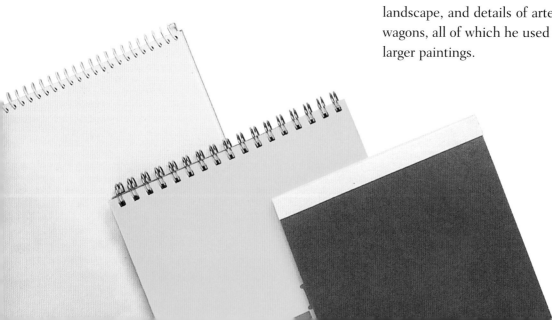

Most drawing media are suitable for quick sketches; selection really depends on personal choice. The speed at which charcoal can be used with little pressure has a certain advantage for the beginner.

Any long journey, or a business or vacation trip, provides the opportunity to sketch unfamiliar places and people. This is

SKETCHBOOK STUDIES

It is no hardship to take your sketchbook with you practically wherever you go. It will provide excellent practice in developing your visual awareness and a valuable source of material for more finished works developed later. In the sketch below, the artist has added written notes that record items of interest about the particular view.

valuable for simple practice in sketching technique, and also forms an interesting personal record of where you have been and what you have seen.

Sketching while you are traveling gives you an occupation for time that might otherwise be wasted. During the hours spent in a car, bus, train, or plane, you can draw the people accompanying you, strangers who are fellow travelers, or the interior of the vehicle itself. There are also snatches of time on any trip when you might be waiting for someone in a lobby or restaurant, or marking time in an unfamiliar hotel room. Then you can use a small sketchbook and a simple tool such as a ballpoint or fiber-tip pen to make quick visual notes.

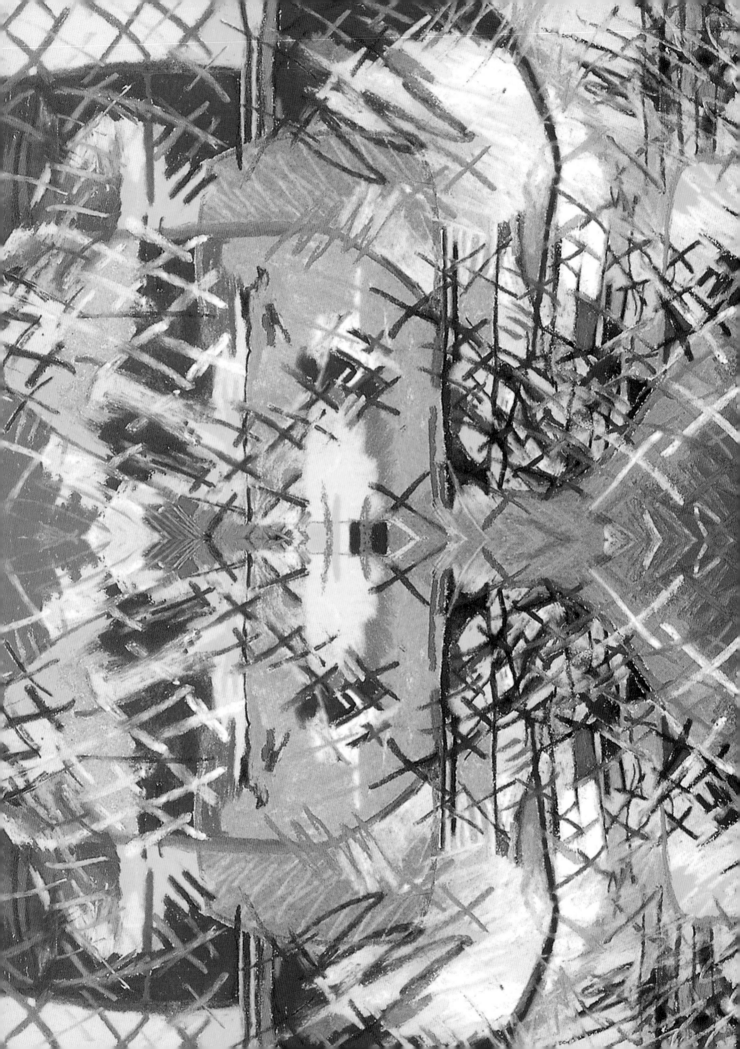

COLOR
AWARENESS

The first stage of any drawing is a line, but to increase its potency we introduce two more elements—tone and color. In essence color is light—light refracted and light absorbed. Without light we see nothing. With it we see an estimated six million colors. Exploring and depicting these colors will not only expand your understanding of reality, but will also train your minds to interpret what is beyond the immediately obvious.

What is color?

Color is an effect of light. The range of colors that we see in a given context depends upon the quality of illumination created by the available light, but the color is a real phenomenon, not an illusory or transient effect. Each material or substance that we perceive as having a particular color is reflecting

THE SPECTRUM

The pigmented representation of the light spectrum illustrates the colors that result when a beam of white light is split into its component parts.

certain light wavelengths and absorbing others, and its ability to do this is inherent. A red object, for example, does not suddenly turn blue under the same light conditions, but it will not appear red if it is not receiving illumination that includes red light wavelengths.

White light contains all colors, and it is under white light that you see what might be called the "true" color of an object—what artists term local color. The spectrum of colored light is estimated to include about 200 pure hues within the visible range, although not all of these are readily distinguishable by the human eye.

For the artist the practical points at issue are the visual sensations of light and color and the ways in which these are experienced. Coloring materials that are solid and textured behave quite differently from colored light. Because white light is composed of colors, a certain combination of colored lights makes white, but with drawing or painting materials, the more colors that are applied, the more colorful or darkly veiled becomes the surface effect. The artist is dealing with substantial elements, and must learn how they can be used to create equivalents of the insubstantial effects of light.

PASTEL WHEEL

The color wheel was devised to explain graphically the relationships of pure hues, showing the three primaries—red, blue, and yellow—linked by the secondary color mixes—purple, green, and orange. Adjacent colors are related, opposite colors are complementary. This example if constructed with strokes of pastel color: it shows the circle of pure hues and also tonal variations from light values in the inner ring to darker tones on the outer border.

COLOR TREE

Colors are divided into different hues. The amount of white or black contained in each color determines its hue. This tree illustrates the main color variations.

The color wheel, linking the six primary color types in a circular formation, is simply a graphic device for explaining the basic relationships of primary and secondary hues. Placing the colors within a segmented circle gives an arrangement in which each primary color faces, in the opposite segment, a secondary that is composed of the other two primaries. Thus by going round the wheel you can identify the relationships of adjacent or harmonious colors, and by working crosswise you can see the opposing pairs of primaries and secondaries known as opposite or complementary colors.

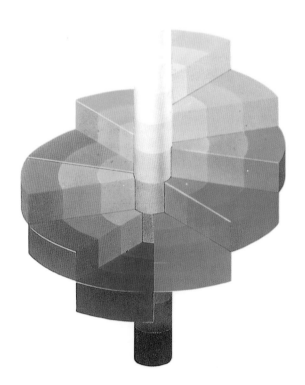

How we see color

GARDEN FLOWERS
by Judy Martin

A large-scale drawing can be a good medium for releasing inhibitions about color work. This image is derived from a display of brilliantly colored garden flowers. Working with both acrylics and pastels, Judy Martin allowed the drawing to develop freely and abstractly.

We see color in physical terms by the action of light on the rods and cones in the retina of the eye. The cones distinguish hues while the rods register qualities of lightness or darkness. By some estimates, a person with normal color vision is capable of identifying up to ten million variations of color values. The conditions known as color blindness include several forms of incomplete color perception—an inability to distinguish red and orange hues from yellow and green is perhaps the most common—and there are rare cases of people who see only in monochrome.

Whatever the scientific evaluation of our visual capacities, none of us can be sure that we see colors in exactly the same way as anyone else. It may be possible to measure the color range of light entering the eye, and to check the efficiency of the physical receptors, but this says nothing of the sensation of color experienced by an individual. Our responses to visual stimuli are "processed" by the brain, which can add memories, associations, and its own inventions to the purely physical information we receive.

JUXTAPOSED COLOR

The yellow–green background acts as a foil to the orange, making it jump forward, whereas the black kills the vibrance of the color.

The color you see in an object is not a flat tone, it is a combination of several colors juxtaposed and interacting with each other. Look at an object carefully, say a white coffee cup. If you study the different parts of it closely you will see not just white and gray, but yellows, blues, and even pinks. An object colored with little tonal variation does not convey as much sense of form as one in which the tones are heightened. We therefore need color to see form.

Any shape you see is a shape of color, created by that color—it is not simply an outline that is "coloured in." Without drawing in outlines it is possible to construct a colored object that looks realistic.

ADVANCING AND RECEDING COLORS

A color's power and its visual dominance are often a direct result of its surrounding color and what the human eye relates it to—if you like, its color context. It is also affected by its volume or area. The panel above illustrates five pairs of colors in reversed positions to show how area and context affect the feeling of a color, making it advance or recede.

Color profiles

Colour interactions are all relative, but gaining a sense of color as an entity in its own right helps to focus your perception of color values in material objects. It is important not to take for granted your response to color or your ability to analyse it in real terms. To begin with, take a look at the the intrinsic character of each color, its sources and associations. The color "profiles" below focus on the origins, range and family characteristics of colors, and are a preparation for considering the more abstract aspects of color relationships.

RED A powerful color— even in small quantities it readily catches the eye, and the brightest and purest hues of red dominate most other colors. The extensive color range of reds passes from the dark-toned, earthy red-browns and rich red-purples to the lighter values of orange-reds and clean, vibrant pinks. Strong reds can have a violent presence, but also an inviting, enveloping density. Red occurs frequently in nature. Original sources of natural red pigments included insect dyes, making crimson and carmine, earth for red ocher, the mineral source of vermilion, cinnabar, and plant dyes providing a range of madders. Modern synthetic pigments have supplemented these natural values of red to create a rich variety.

ORANGE Standing between red and yellow in the color spectrum, orange is secondary to both these colors and shares some of their visual characteristics and emotional impact. Its values readily merge into yellow, red, or shades of warm brown, leaving true orange as a color of relatively limited character. Yet natural orange hues seen in fruits, flowers and foliage, minerals, gemstones, and warmly colored metals such as copper and bronze are rich and various. There have been few good natural sources of pigment or dye, and orange is usually a "manufactured" color, yet it is commonly associated with elemental resources such as energy, warmth, and light.

YELLOW This color occupies a narrower band of the spectrum of colored light than the others. It is highly reflective and naturally light-toned, providing a sense of illumination. Whereas most colors will darken with increasing saturation, yellow tends to appear brighter as it gains intensity. The words used to describe different qualities of pure yellow are taken from natural contexts—sunshine yellow, lemon yellow, golden yellow. Earth colors such as yellow ocher and raw sienna represent the darker values, but the darker, heavier tones tend to "slip

out" of the yellow family, to be categorized as light browns or muddy greens. When there is a strong bias toward another hue, yellow is quickly perceived instead as pale orange or citrus green, depending on the particular bias.

GREEN It is impossible to dissociate green from the idea of life and growth in nature, but in fact there are few natural sources of green pigment, and the many values of green coloring agents, including those used in artists' materials, have been chemically developed. In physical terms, the eye focuses green easily and it is thought to be a restful color, a sensation underlined by its perceived naturalness. Green hues are extremely various, beginning with those close to yellow at one end of the range and ending with rich blue-greens at the other. Like the yellows, the true greens are given descriptive names from nature such as emerald green, grass green, sap green.

BLUE As a primary color and one with a strong presence and a wide range of hues and tones, blue tends to rival reds for dominance, showing little of the influence of other primary or secondary hues. Dark and light values of blue are often equal in intensity to its pure hues. An inevitable association with natural elements credits blue with qualities of airiness, coolness, and peace, but it is also a vivid and decorative color in nature, seen in some of its richest tones in flower colors and flashing out from the otherwise dull plumage of some common birds, effects quite different from the pervasive clear blues of open sky. Lapis lazuli, the original source of ultramarine, was a rare and valued mineral pigment, and other blues came from plant dyes such as woad and indigo, but synthetic pigments have greatly increased the range.

PURPLE A secondary, or mixed color, purple combines properties of blue and red, the strongest primaries, so it can provide a powerfully rich color sensation. The color range includes hues that we describe as purple, violet, or mauve, each suggesting a slightly different quality. Violet is represented in the spectrum of colored light. Purples, of limited availability from natural sources, are typically manufactured colors that did not figure largely in the artist's palette until the late nineteenth century. Purple itself is a naturally dark-toned color, light purples usually being achieved by mixing with white. The word mauve suggests softer shades with a bias toward the gentler reds, such as carmine, madder, and the paler pinks, while descriptions such as lilac or lavender, used as color names, are purely associative.

ACHROMATIC COLORS Chroma is the quality of "colorfulness" in colors. Black, white, and pure grays are described as achromatic, having in theory no color bias. In terms of color science, black is the result of all colors in light being absorbed by a surface. White results from the total reflection of all colors, and a neutral gray is seen when all wavelengths of light are absorbed to an equal degree. In real terms, there is usually three to five percent inefficiency in the absorption or reflection of light, so we are often able to distinguish different qualities of whiteness, blackness, or grayness that also include a hint of color value.

Creating your own color

In most painting media, the colors are pre-mixed and then applied to the working surface, but in the case of colored pencils the colors must be created on the surface itself. The medium thus necessitates careful analysis on the way the color is made up in any subject, since by applying several pure pigments to a surface in order to build up a secondary color, you are in effect re-constructing the component elements of the color perceived.

Pencil pigment is semi-opaque, which means that a multitude of colors can be created by layering them in varying amounts and pressures. When developing these colors it is important to remember that you are drawing shape, mood, life, and scale with each color depicted. Do not fall into the trap of seeing your subject as either a monotone composition to which you add color, or

TONAL RANGE WITH THREE PIGMENTS

The mixed colors, right, show how a dramatic range of color can be created using only three basic pigments. Despite the translucent nature of colored pencil pigment, some colors will dominate others according to their natural intensity—for example, red dominates yellow, and black dominates most colors.

COLOR GRADATIONS

Two sets of color gradations—warm yellow to red and warm yellow to cool blue—are illustrated below. The left-hand column in each set was achieved using considerable pressure on the pencil, and the right-hand column was created using very little pressure.

a group of shades or outlines that have to be filled in with color. Color is the essence of your work—it is neither superficial nor an afterthought!

In creating colors with pencils you are actively mixing pigment and developing blends of hue, intensity, lightness, and darkness. There is a basic palette of colors that is necessary to re-create the colors of light. But because light and pigment do not fully correlate in their color-mixing properties it is necessary to develop a palette of colored pigments that will visually achieve the same effects as those of light.

BLENDING COLORS

The swatches of color, above, illustrate the huge range of blended colors that can be created on the paper, and how colors change when laid over others. From left to right, green, yellow, orange, blue, and red were laid. Colored over them, front top to bottom, were red, orange, magenta, light blue, dark blue, brown, light green, and dark green.

TECHNIQUE

Techniques in any creative work are largely dictated by the characteristics of your chosen medium. For instance, drawing with coloured pencils involves a gradual building process, without which you cannot develop blocks of colour and complex mixed-colour effects. The important thing is to become familiar with the properties of your materials and the ways in which these can be used to recreate your visual impression of the chosen subject.

Strokes

A drawn line or stroke may be the most elementary statement, but it is nonetheless one of the most important and emotive marks in artistic impression. It is quite useful to practice making several strokes to investigate their potential. Far from stating the obvious, it is an exercise in working a pencil in order for you to be able to handle it, understand it, and feel through it, to create your desired effect. It is the rapport between your hand, your pencil, and the paper that will enable you to create a physical impression of your mental image. The degree of control that you have over this facility will, in the end, affect the degree of versatility and the range of effect you will achieve—if you like, the palette of your abilities.

PENCIL LEADS

The difference in the texture of pencil leads creates quite different lines, above. The pencil on the left has a pastel consistency and so produces a very smudgy, textured line. Similarly, the watercolor pencil on the right has a soft lead that makes a thick line. The pencil in the center has a very hard lead, which creates a thin, consistent line.

STROKES AND TEXTURE

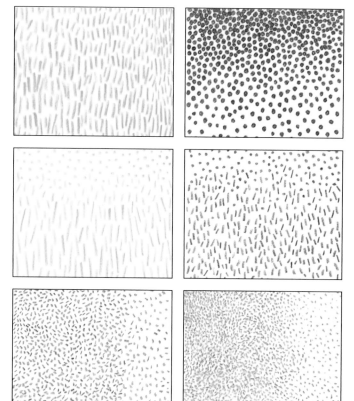

The blocks of marks show how very simple strokes can produce a huge range of surface patterns and textures with their own shape and directional statements. Top left, a regular, more or less vertical, pattern is produced with short lines of similar line length. Top right, by twisting the point of the pencil on the paper, very even dots can be created that suggest tone, and by varying the density of their distribution it is possible to suggest lighter or darker color. Center left, dots becoming short lines create a sense of movement and direction. Center right, very short consistent lines produced a stippled, almost prickly, texture. Bottom left, very short lines applied in a random direction create a harsher texture than the dots do. Bottom right, by shortening strokes and increasing their density a sense of shadow can be produced.

Before you start to make a stroke it is important to consider what type of effect you require, because this will determine your choice of materials. For instance, if you compare a number of pencils, you will see that the leads have different qualities—hard or soft, smooth or crumbly. These qualities will be heightened depending on the type of paper surface you use. It is important to experiment with a variety of drawing surfaces such as watercolor paper, machine-textured paper, and gesso boards to discover your favorite materials and the right pencils for them. Try buying a variety of textured papers in sheet form and draw a simple area of line and tone over each, using the same pencil throughout. This will soon illustrate the influence of the surface on the range of effects that you can achieve.

Having decided what type of pencil you want to use, it is important to ascertain its "crumble factor." This will dictate, or at least help you to decide, how to sharpen the pencil, which is of paramount importance in determining the type of line you will achieve. It is easy to maintain a fairly sharp point with a hard lead, whereas many softer leads tend to crumble if too much lead is exposed from the wood, or if the sharpener does not reduce the lead gradually. A standard pencil sharpener will produce a reasonably even, rounded point, but for other effects you should experiment with a craft knife, Stanley knife, or a scalpel.

LINE QUALITY

The strokes shown at the bottom left of this page show how the width of pencil lines is affected by the way you hold the pencil—underhand, underhand and rolling the pencil, or overhand. The strokes below right were drawn with various pressures and differ in shape, width, and tone.

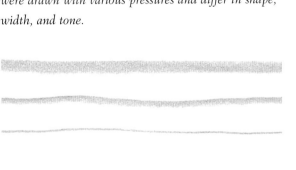

CREATING TEXTURE AND FORM WITH LINES

Above, patches of strokes, some short, some long, applied with varying pressure, convey accurately the rough, broken texture of bricks.

DRAWING DOTS

Drawing dots is a good point at which to start in your investigation of strokes. Dots may be produced simply by banging the point of the pencil on the surface. Again, the leads will vary in their reaction to this treatment, providing a range of marks from precise pin-pricks to smudgy spots.

Once dots grow into short lines, they inherit a natural direction—usually that in which they are drawn. Open scribbling works in a similar way to hatching, but is a more fluid process since you do not lift the drawing tool in making he lines, and they remain loosely connected. The method enables you to exploit the sense of movement in the drawn lines to express rhythms and tensions. The gestural quality of marks depends on the movement of the line and the scale in which it is incorporated.

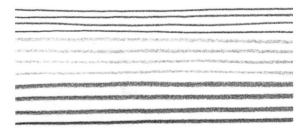

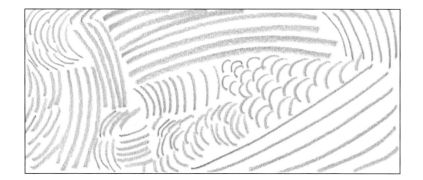

By applying strokes quickly in patches of exaggerated curves, longer strokes and shorter, slightly curved lines, a busy, turbulent pattern is created.

CURVED STROKES

Once the length of your line begins to grow it will develop a curvature. Because of the way in which the arm moves the body from left to right, or the other way, an arc-shaped gesture results. It is therefore quite natural that long lines should follow this sweeping curved movement. Because we tend to draw the finger and thumb inward when moving the pencil from top to bottom, or alternatively pivot the hand when taking the pencil from left to right (or right to left), we again create a curved line. Curved lines are a natural development from the creation of almost static dots or very short lines, and only through conscious effort and the use of rulers do we manage to keep lines straight.

Curved lines offer an added dimension within linework to create a sensation of movement and depth. They may be used in a static sense, depicting the shape of a curved surface by running in a similar direction; they may also be used individually or in small blocks, running in opposite directions to create a very complex texture. If the

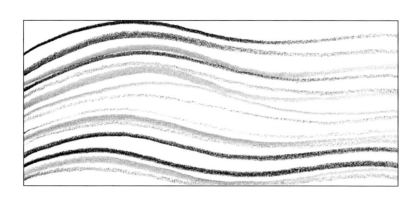

Long fluid lines that ripple slightly still convey movement and direction but the sense of speed is slow and the feeling, one of tranquility. By varying the density and thickness of the strokes you can emphasize dimension.

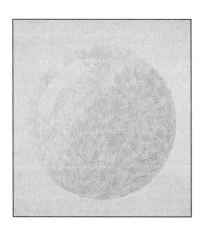
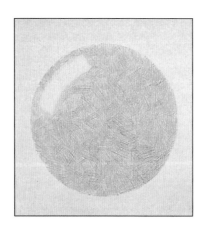

width of the line remains constant then a purely two-dimensional texture will be created, but if this width varies from thick to thin then the eye will not only be led around the subject but will also travel into and out of the image, adding a three-dimensional characteristic to simple linework.

Curved lines can also suggest movement or speed. Again, the fluctuating width of the line with substantiate the effect of moving from front to back or from left to right. Rapidly drawn, short curved lines will imply a quick movement, whereas long, gentle sweeping lines will insinu-ate slow, smooth movement. Experiment in one color to produce these various effects, then do the same exercise using a combination of colors and observe how colors such as red and yellow heighten the effect. Try also running curved lines in parallel, either as long strokes or as short controlled patches. Then compare them with curved lines flowing generally in a similar direction, but drawn at random, and with curved lines drawn over each other in a completely ad hoc fashion.

The complexity of statements you can make with strokes is infinite.

PENCIL DRAWING
by Judy Martin

The basic lines in this drawing give an overall impression of a dense woodland. The pencil sketch was made in front of the original subject and the color detail is a studio reworking of the theme based on selected elements of the pencil version.

STROKES AND FORM

These five illustrations, left, show the development of a color, a shape, and a three-dimensional form, using groups of short, straight strokes. The shape develops as layer upon layer of linework build up the color. In each layer the lines criss-cross in a similar pattern, leaving white space in areas of high color and becoming denser in areas of shadow. In the final picture a flat background is drawn in the same style.

Hatching

Hatching is one of the most commonly used methods of creating blocks of color and tone in drawing. Hatching is the technique of drawing one group of lines in a given direction and overlaying or overlapping another group of lines in a different direction. When these two sets of lines run in almost opposite directions, in a cross-like manner, the pattern created is known as cross-hatching. Cross-hatching builds a more densely woven textural effect that can be varied by spacing the lines openly or close together and varying the angle of their crossing.

Hatching can be very neat and precise, or very loose and emphatic. It has a directional emphasis according to how you form the strokes, and this can be manipulated to create the effect of changing planes and curves in describing solid form.

CRAB
by Jan McKenzie

In this convincingly detailed color rendering, the almost solid color areas in the background and the crab shell are mainly developed through hatching and cross-hatching. In some areas, oil pastel has been scratched through with the point of a light-colored pencil to lift the tonal values.

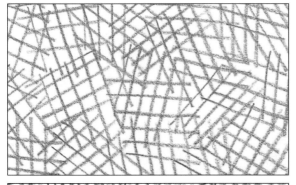

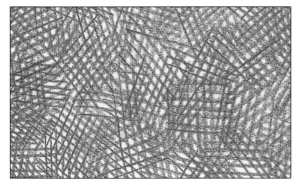

CROSS-HATCHED PATTERN

When creating cross-hatched patterns it is important to determine how the lines will fit together and how they will appear in the scale of your work. Top, the lines are so widely spaced that the white gaps predominate—to provide texture and color they would be more appropriate for a larger space. Center, the grid is more balanced—it lends color to the white spaces and its texture is more effective. Bottom, the lines carry more weight than the spaces do, creating more pronounced color.

The lines may be thick and heavy, creating a dense texture; alternatively they may be thin and fine reflecting a highly controlled, delicate and precise rendering. Any effect that you can achieve in a single line can be heightened and duplicated by placing similar textural marks over or alongside it, offering great scope to create dimensional forms and surfaces on paper. Investigate the color possibilities by drawing a simple hatched gray scale. Compare this to the gray scale you might create with flat tone, and the textural depth of the cross-hatched area will be self-evident. Try also applying this scale of tone to a three-dimensional object and you will see just how strong a sense of color is possible using hatching rather than a flatter, gradated tone.

In drawing, cross-hatching has a slightly architectural quality, well suited to depicting structural forms, but it does not preclude softer, more fluid versions for depicting less hard or animate objects.

HATCHING AND TEXTURE

Hatching techniques have been used for centuries as a drawing device and were particularly successful used by engravers, who developed an enormous repertoire of tonal values by building up areas of hatching and cross-hatching from a simple, rather harsh, straight line. Both techniques have also been widely used to create a sense of "color," form, and texture in a monochrome work. When using one color, a sense of tone can be created only increasing or decreasing the area of white within the colored surface. This can be seen easily in the gradation of a pencil tone over a medium-grained surface. However, by hatching or cross-hatching with color, a more varied and complex pattern of color density is achievable.

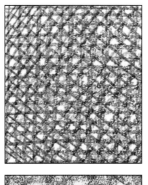
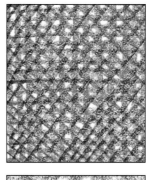

Cross-hatching over different surfaces often produces a change in emphasis of color, as demonstrated in these examples in which the same colors were used, applied in the same direction, but on different papers.

The same pencils were used to create the examples, but the different papers used affected the color of the cross-hatching produced.

In repeating one line alongside another and in drawing one gridlike pattern over another, a vast array of "surfaces" may be created. The specific qualities of the surface will be governed by the type of pencil used, its point, the type of paper, the degrees of pressure applied and the resultant line character. The distance apart that the lines are placed will also have distinct effects on the density and texture of the tone created. The eye will read not only the lines drawn but the gaps between them as well, thus producing an effect of negative and positive visual sensation. When the lines are close together they will be dominant, and their "edge" will create texture; when the lines are far apart the gaps will be dominant, the pencil line bordering the shapes.

DIFFERENT PENCIL POINTS

The two cross-hatched areas, left, differ in their density only. The patch at the top appears considerably lighter in color than the one below it, although equal pressure has been used on both samples. The difference lies in the way that the pencil leads were sharpened. The precise point of the pencil in the top image has produced crisp lines but in the second image the lead has been allowed to develop several facets that have created a softer, heavier line.

By overlaying lines at a given point, or visually bending them by placing curved lines over straight lines, the strength of composition of a surface can also be hinted at. Experiment by placing one group of parallel lines over another, starting with a simple grid pattern on paper. Draw a duplicate on tracing paper and place it over the original pattern. By turning the tracing gradually through 180 degrees you will see the wide range of effects achievable in simple hatching. These will range from solid strong textures formed from the overlaying of a number of grids of different dimensions at a variety of angles, in order to create a wider range of color density and surface pattern, to a number of optical illusions that may prove useful in describing shape, when a gridlike pattern is drawn at an oblique angle over a perfectly square grid. The result of this method will be the appearance of a curve in the straight lines where none actually exists.

By varying the distance apart of the lines on one of the grids or by using a different lead and placing a tight fine grid over a thick crumbly grid, further textures will be created. Then experiment by drawing curved lines and overlay these on a straight grid pattern. The effect of a static or moving texture will develop that may be further enhanced by the colors used.

BUILDING UP COLOR

The color swatches above show a sequence of cross-hatching in which only four colors—yellow, orange, red, and blue—are used. It is usual to build up color from the palest tone to the darkest, thereby allowing scope for adjustment before the color becomes too dark. The dominance of colors can be seen in these samples where the red completely overrides the grid formed in red, yellow, and orange.

HATCHED SHADOW

Hatching is extremely effective for depicting shadow areas where many reflected colors overlap. Using delicate grids of hatched lines, layers of pure pigment are allowed to shine through to create a complex color interpretation.

Sgraffito

Sgraffito is the eighteenth-century word to describe an artistic treatment that has been in existence since the earliest efforts to communicate through drawing. It refers to the incising, or scratching of lines into a surface, often taking the form of cutting through layers of color to reveal others beneath.

When you are creating a drawing, there are a number of ways in which you can create surface texture in the work. Texture on the image is an added dimension, equal in importance to the texture of the paper used, the texture of your chosen media, and the texture depicted. Sgraffito can be either incorporated early in the laying of colors, or used as a finishing technique.

TOOLS AND THEIR MARKS

There is almost no end to the type of instrument that you can use to incise lines into compact pigment. The most commonly used tools are a pair of scissors, a Stanley knife, a scalpel, a designer's knife, a pair of dividers, a razor blade and pins, but the choice is down to you.

Practice laying down heavy amounts of colored pigment on varying rough and smooth surfaces, using a number of mixed colors, and experiment with layering the color, applying the lightest tone first and finishing with a dark top coat, and vice versa. Then practice removing the pigment with different sharp tools without cutting into the base. This is easier said than done and will take a considerable amount of patience to avoid damaging the paper surface.

SGRAFFITO MARKS

Two different surfaces—CS10 board (right) and hardboard primed with gesso (left)—illustrate a range of incised marks to demonstrate the importance of the surface in determining the type of line achieved.

The type of instrument used to create the scratchlike marks, and the way and angle in which the instrument is held, will determine both the style of the mark and the ease with which it is made.

Cutting through a dark color to reveal lighter colors beneath will give an etched effect and can offer a precision in depicting very fine colored lines that is unmatched by any other method. Surface patterns—from fine pin-pricks through to soft graded scrapes of color—and surface textures, may be developed to add dimension to otherwise flat color.

THE BLUE GATE
by Milton Meyer

Sgraffito can be used for a wide variety of textures, but is especially appropriate for wood grain. In this pastel drawing of a farmhouse in Galway, the artist has used the technique very cleverly on the gates in the foreground of the picture.

Try using a long scalpel blade (which will bend fairly easily) to pick into the surface, creating sharp, pointed, little marks. Then use the side of the blade or a mounted razor blade to sweep across an area of colored pigment, removing a fine, colored "dust" very gradually to reveal the layers beneath. You will be able to create very smooth pale hues by removing concentrated pigment in this way—the knife edge not only takes off the excess color particles but also, by means of pressure, refines and blends what remains.

Sgraffito is an excellent method of creating dimension, be it for surface pattern generally, or specific areas of a drawing. It is certainly a technique of reduction, where less becomes more. Remember that its success lies in you thinking in reverse, building up colored layers in the order of their removal.

PAPER SURFACE AND PIGMENT DENSITY

The surface of the paper and the density and thickness of the pencil pigment are of great importance in the end result of a sgraffito drawing. The quality and definition of the line, whether it is a short, "picked" stroke, a hatched or cross-hatched line or a long, fine cut, are greatly enhanced or reduced by these two factors.

Burnishing

Burnishing is a surface technique used to create added dimension to a work both in terms of finish and color. It is a method of blending color through pressure, and in its simplest form may be the result of fusing two colors by rubbing steadily over them with a tortillon, or paper stump, until they are literally ground down. This technique relies on reducing the pigment particles deposited on the paper to a fine grain and pushing them into the surface texture, resulting in a smooth, almost shiny finish. Because it does impart a gloss to the surface of the drawing it is often used to finish details that are shiny in character or to draw objects made from reflective materials, such as metal or ceramics.

Burnishing with colored pencils is often more successful when carried out with a white or pale gray pencil. Moving a pencil vigorously back and forth over colored areas burnishes in the pigments, allowing the color itself to be altered. At the same time it offers a method with which to create very precise blending in controllable areas. Burnishing can also be very effective in producing highlight areas. Burnishing can also be very effective in producing highlight effects by giving an edge to an area of matt surface.

Experiment with swatches of color, both pure and mixed, to test burnishing with a tortillon, or a white or gray pencil. Alternatively, if a very soft, colored pencil is used, a similar effect can be achieved using an eraser over the penciled surface, although this will tend to produce a more smudged effect. A drawback in using an eraser in this way is that it quickly becomes contaminated with the excess pigment that it picks up and

BURNISHING WITH WHITE, GRAY, AND OCHER

The demonstration, right, shows four colors, each burnished with white, gray, and ocher. Any color, when burnished, will adopt the hue of the color laid over it. The colors here indicate the variety of effects that these three neutral tones can create and reveal that the color change that these tones render on one pigment is not necessarily the same when applied to other colors.

The ability of white to blend or change colors when burnished on top of them is quite apparent when seen over a range of pigments, top of page 55.

unless you rub off the pigment on the eraser, its use on other areas of the drawing is restricted.

Burnishing is particularly effective over areas of gradated tone and where areas of white are to be bordered by color, as in reflections. Look at shiny objects and concentrate on their highlights. Working from this point outward add color and shape. Once you have laid the basic pigment, again, working from the highlight area, burnish gradually with short, intense strokes outward until the whole object is treated in the same way. Remember that the relatively extreme pressure that this technique requires is not really suitable for papers with a heavy surface, because the pressure will either break up the paper's finish, will wrinkle, or even tear it under such stress.

BURNISHING WITH WHITE

Colors change when overlaid with white (*above right*), and it is a useful experiment to observe the differences created when overlaying a color with white. Laying a base of white pigment over which color is laid will act as a reflector to the color and will increase its intensity, whereas overlaying white on color will tend to mute strong colors, making them "chalky" in appearance.

HIGHLIGHTING

Burnishing may be integrated into the plan of a drawing but can easily be utilized as an afterthought to highlight a particular element or intro-

duce a new texture to the surface of the picture. It can also be used as a technique in itself to create texture, such as shiny lines over a matt surface, or glassy dots on a plain background. Taking this principle further it is possible to alter the entire nature of a flat-toned work by burnishing over the whole surface of the completed piece with a particular movement. In so doing you can create a stroke-like texture over the surface of a drawing that bears no relation to the drawing—you can literally apply a finish!

BURNISHING IMPLEMENTS

The examples, left, show the different effects that a variety of burnishing implements will achieve. Far left, the tortillon offers a very controlled, highly pressured burnish, whereas the eraser, centre, produces softer, smudged strokes. Right, the effect of white crayon is seen most clearly where little or no paper shows through.

Impressed line

There may be times when you want to produce a slightly different texture, either to pull out and raise delicate details in your image, or for an overall effect to heighten the color and life in your drawing. Interesting results can be obtained in a number of ways to modify the color and textural qualities of your given surface, by embossing the paper. The techniques fall into two main categories, resulting either positive or negative texture. Neither texture can be created with damp paper or with water-soluble pencils.

There are certain types of paper that respond better than others to embossing techniques; these tend to be raggy and fairly soft. Very hard papers or papers with "china" surfaces have a highly-compacted fibrous structure and do not "give" as easily. But experimentation is the only way to push a paper to its limits, so try out all types of paper.

With positive texture you alter the entire surface quality of the paper by raising the level of the surface. A resilient but fairly soft paper will

STILL LIFE WITH ONIONS

The striations on the translucent layers of onion skin are an ideal pattern to depict using impressed line. The artist traced the outline of the onions and their markings on tracing paper laid over the final drawing surface, pressing hard with a graphite pencil.

react best to this technique. Taking a textured surface such as a heavily grained piece of wood, or a brick, hold your paper over the texture and rub gradually over the paper surface to impress the underlying texture into your paper. This can be done prior to adding color, using a smooth metal-tipped or plastic burnisher, or it can be done in conjunction with laying the color, by the pressured action of the colored pencil. Various

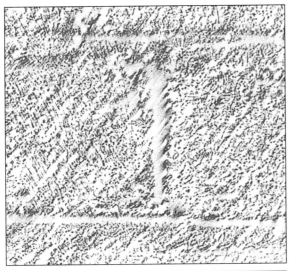

FROTTAGE AND IMPRESSED LINE

On the left are two examples of creating texture by rubbing color over paper on different surfaces. The top illustration was done over a brick wall and the sample below was colored over fabric. This technique can produce a rich and unusual effect, particularly when the layers of colors are burnished over a variety of surfaces. The degree of pressure exerted by the pencil point can be altered to create still more subtle effects.

papers will react in different ways to the textures they are placed on and to the subsequent treatment that they are given and it is advisable to experiment. Do, however, use a gentle pressure to begin with, especially with a burnisher, and gradually build up the weight of your strokes and, ultimately, the depth of the texture.

The technique that gives you a negative texture is particularly useful, enabling you to create very precise, fine, white linework within a colored area, something that is quite difficult to achieve. White seldom remains pure in colored pencil works because the pigment is semi-opaque and, however, it is applied, color will show through it even if it is only an off-white effect from the paper used. White pencils also have a habit of becoming tinted, by picking up colored pigments, or producing tinted effects from their proximity to color, which can reduce the clarity of the image.

The only way to ensure a pure white line is to create a negative line that lies beneath the surface of the paper and remains clean while pigment is being applied on top. This is a negative or impressed line. It is simple to use, quick and clean, and the result can be stunning.

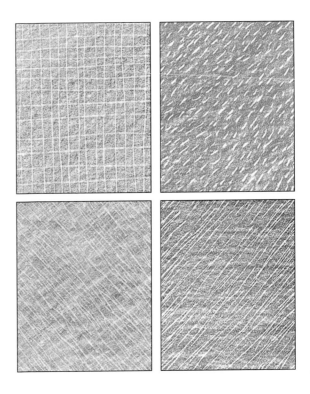

METHODS OF IMPRESSED LINE

Line can be impressed into paper with any number of sharp objects drawing over a sheet of paper laid on top of the actual drawing surface. Top left the marks were made with a pencil and top right with the artist's finger nail. Bottom left, lines were impressed into paper and then a layer of orange was laid over it. Bottom right, lines were impressed into the paper and covered with layers of dark blue. Each layer had lines impressed into it so that the end result is one of many lines texturing the pigment.

GETTING IT RIGHT

Any aspiring artist is well advised to try to come to terms with as much theory as possible. By looking at reproductions in books and visiting galleries you will be able to compare the ways in which various artists have dealt with problems of composition and perspective. Perhaps the most useful method, however, of learning about these subjects is through your own work. By setting yourself exercises and trying to complete them in the light of what you have read and observed you will gradually acquire greater understanding and be able to put this to practical use.

Planning the composition

In drawing you have two main factors under your control: the viewpoint you choose and the materials you decide to use. If, as we are assuming in this section of the book, the main aim of your drawing is to record what you see, this places certain limits on the expressive and interpretive qualities of your drawing. For example, if you are working on a still life of objects standing against a blue background, you would not suddenly decide to change the background color in the drawing to red because you feel it might make a better picture. This would completely alter the relative color values and pictorial mood of the image that, although a valid approach to drawing, is inappropriate to a representational image. If you are using the subject as a direct model for a color drawing, it is up to you to decide beforehand whether a blue or red background will create the best effect.

A still life provides you with a wide range of choices that include the general forms and colors of the setting as well as those of the objects used to assemble the arrangement. The same applies to a posed figure. The model can be positioned in a particular place to be framed by, say, a window, a mirror or a flatly colored wall; furniture, draperies, and props such as plants or ornaments can be introduced to vary the shapes, colors, and patterns within the overall design, and you can arrive at a pleasing composition before you start to draw.

In a landscape or townscape view, there are fewer ways of manipulating the combination of elements, and in any case, it is the actuality of what you see that attracts you to the subjects in the first place.

OLIVE TREES
by Judith Rothchild

In her pastel drawing of an olive tree set against the landscape of Malaga, the artist places the tree at the center of the composition but, rather than appearing to divide the image, the curved trunk and branching crown form a sinuous link between landscape and sky. The colors and tones are carefully judged to capture the character of the landscape, the detail of natural and architectural forms, and the brilliant sunlight illuminating the view. This is achieved by the complete integration of patterns of light and shade across the local colors of the landscape.

COMPOSING AN IMAGE

Thumbnail sketches are an essential starting point for any decisions on composition, from the points of view of both form and color. Explore the possible variations by altering the amounts of background or foreground included, and by placing the focal point of the work at the left and right side of the composition. In the example, below, the verticality of the vase of flowers is balanced by the horizontal expanse of the window. In the second image, below, the artist decides to use the angles of the corner of the room and the table in contrast to the cylindrical form of the vase.

Below left, by cropping in on the sides and emphasizing the vertical feeling of the image, the vase of tulips is made to dominate the composition. By taking a viewpoint farther back and bringing in the edge of the table, below, the centrally placed vase is integrated more fully into its environment and the composition.

Here your methods of controlling the composition and "setting up the image" are limited to the scale of the drawing, the part of the view you select to draw, and the viewpoint from which you observe it. You have to find the particular viewpoint from which the subject is seen at its most descriptive, whereas with a smaller-scale subject you may be free to select and arrange the elements as you please.

Viewpoint is always a definitive factor in composition. Often the first impression of a view or an interesting object stimulates your mind's eye to form an idea of a drawn image. But this doesn't always mean that the exact position from which you first saw the subject is the ideal one. On closer examination you may see some aspect that is slightly disruptive—an ugly shape or a block of jarring color—which could be modified if you moved your position to left or right. A slight shift of position may provide a more balanced or a more complex image, or you might decide to take an angle of view that enhances a

LANDSCAPE COMPOSITION

You can see that by altering the position of the picture plane the composition of this painting is altered. In photography every time you point your camera in a slightly different direction at the same landscape you are altering the camera's picture plane and you will therefore take

a different photograph. The artist's eye, when working in a representational manner, is reacting to the landscape in a similar way to the camera. Use a simple frame to help you decide upon the most stimulating picture plane for any scene.

One of the purposes of color drawing may be to develop a composition for interpretation in another medium. This drawing by Elisabeth Harden was a preparation for a lithograph. On the basis of a deliberately restricted color range, the artist used this drawing to work out the general form of the composition and the way in which the colors could be overprinted in lithography.

characteristic element of the subject. By moving closer to some tall buildings, for example, taking a viewpoint that forces you to look upward a little, you will be emphasizing height in the perspective of the drawing.

LOCAL COLOR

The color of an object or material under white light—the color it naturally reflects—is known as its local color. the bright mid-green of a leaf, the yellow-green of an apple, red rose petals, a blue vase, an orange book cover—in each of these descriptions, the color is the local color of the object. It is a means of identification, part of the information that helps us to recognize things by their inherent properties.

Local color is modified by a number of things: the quality of illumination: the object's surface texture; hints of other colors reflected from the surroundings. In an open landscape view, atmospheric effects of distance or weather conditions will alter local color.

ESTABLISHING A COMPOSITION

The simplest way to map out a composition is to deal with each component as a characteristic outline or block shape. As explained earlier, it is important to think in terms of color from the earliest stages, and a good way to begin is to establish the viewpoint and and general design of the image by drawing outlines or block shapes using only the local colors of each element of your chosen subject. For the time being ignore the tonal contrasts of light and shade and the complexities of pattern and texture, and concentrate on individual shapes. Look at their relationships as flat elements on the picture plane, working in terms of their arrangement within the "frame" of the drawing paper.

Rapid sketches in colored pencil give a good general impression of different compositional arrangements. The horizon level is kept constant: the horizontal stress of the landscape can be emphasized or opposed, with points of focus traveling along the horizon line or breaking through it.

Perception

You will probably think it strange that the first thing it is suggested you do in a book about drawing is to write something, but it is essential to be aware of how we use our eyes in the everyday business of conducting our lives, and to discover what adjustments we have to make to our perceptual processes to successfully make representational drawings.

As an exercise, perhaps at the end of an evening meal, leave the dining table and walk into the adjoining room. Write a full description of the table you have just left. It will probably containing the following sort of information:

"There are four dinner plates on the table, knives and forks, water-jug, coffee cups, drinking glasses. The table is a round, mahogany table."

This first description will probably be quite limited, constructed almost as a list enumerating the various items you can remember.

Now return to the room you were in. Sit looking at the table in front of you and write another description. You will probably discover there are quite a few things that you had left out. The reason for suggesting that you carry out both of these descriptions is simply to make you use your eyes.

You can see from these two photographs that they have been taken from different angles. It is obvious that the photographs are of the same table, but the visual information they contain is very different. This is even more apparent when the two photographs are transformed into two line drawings (right).

*This pencil drawing was obviously done
from memory but by an untutored eye.
Little attempt has been made to render the
drawing with any perspective, even though
the objects that were listed are all in place.*

The difficulty arises, however, when you try to translate this method of observation into a drawing. Most beginners find it exceedingly difficult a table from wherever they are viewing it. It is impossible to see it as a complete circle, and there is a strong compulsion to visually tilt the surface so that all the objects you wish to drawn can be clearly seen, as in the drawing above. This is not due to any lack of ability to see, but to use the information seen in a way that is not compatible with the act of drawing, but that corresponds completely with the act of verbal description.

The next exercise is to draw the table, first placing a chair about eight or ten feet away, sit down and try to draw the objects on the table from this one fixed viewpoint. It soon becomes apparent that not all the objects on the table can be fully seen. One object may by partly obscured by a chair that is in your line of vision. You will probably still find that you tend to draw one object first in its entirety, then move on to the next, and so on, and that you try to fit the table and chairs round the objects.

The main problem most beginners have in perceiving the interrelationship of all the objects is thus due in some degree to the fact that they tend to perceive the world in a solely three-dimensional way. The exercises in this book are designed to help you start asking yourself the right questions, through your eyes. Learn by the experience of drawing from life, and do not expect to be able to comprehend all the aspects of drawing right from the beginning.

Perspective

LANDSCAPE
by Jane Strother

Natural features of the landscape often provide strong cues for the arrangement of a composition. In this view, the artist makes use of the linear pattern of a plantation to lead the viewer from the foreground of the picture into the horizontal spread of the middle ground. There is an interesting perspective in the undulations of the land and the artist has selected a relatively high viewpoint.

Aerial or color perspective is a device that has been used for centuries by painters to enhance pictorial depth and the sense of distance in landscape compositions. Unlike linear perspective, which depends on scale and contour to develop spatial relationships, aerial perspective is an effect derived from particular perceptions of tonal and color values. In the foreground of a landscape, colors are at their brightest and most intense, the tonal contrasts are at their most emphatic. As the image recedes into the middle distance the definition becomes less pronounced and the range of color values diminishes, narrowing in the far distance to a scale consisting mainly of blues and grays.

Details of form are also gradually eliminated so that the background elements are presented in terms of broad masses lacking distinct and individual features.

You can see this occurring in an extensive landscape view. It is an optical effect caused by vapors and particles that hang in the air and, with increasing distance, create a "veil" that softens the edge qualities, surface textures, and color and tonal contrasts. The convention has been used successfully in images ranging in style from meticulously realist to broadly impressionistic. It illustrates the general principle that color relationships contribute significantly to pictorial definition of space and form.

If we look at this idea in greater detail, we can see it in terms of a more abstract idea of color interactions. A flat area of a single color creates no particular spatial sense, but as soon as we add a second color or a different tone of the same color there is an immediate tension, which begins to suggest a spatial relationship. This may be an effect of light and dark tonal values—the lighter color seeming to advance from the darker; or one of warm and cool contrast—a strong,

VICTORIAN RAILWAY STATION

A pencil and wash study of a glass roof of a Victorian railway station, London. This drawing relies upon a painstaking control of perspective as well as silhouette to create a cavernous expanse of glass and steel.

CITY VIEW
by Ian Ribbons

Ian Ribbons captures the somber mood of a city view using neutral grays and browns merging into yellows, greens, and blues. The perspective of the composition leads the eye into the shadowed center of the image from where the activity of the busy streets fans out on either side. Contrasted areas of light and dark tone enhance the sense of space and structure.

deep red, for example, forcing it way out from a cool mid-blue. It may be the way an intense color interacts with a somber one, as with a brilliant sunshine yellow flashing across a muddy ocher. In general, it can be said that contrasts create space, while evenly balanced hues and tones tend to compete for spatial dominance.

There is also, of course, a structure within a composition—created by contrasts between linear elements and mass, or the relative scale and interplay of shapes. To produce a naturalistic rendering, you need to make the color values work with the other formal elements of the composition. If you arrange colors and tones to act against the framework of the pictorial space, you are reinterpreting the image in a non-objective way that acts to flatten depth and form. These

EXPERT TIP

The theory of perspective is quite complex, and even if you work to its formulae, it is often necessary to provide optical "correction" to a drawing so that the image corresponds to normal perception rather than to a set of pictorial rules. However, it may be helpful to be aware that there is a perspective element in both large- and small-scale subjects.

effects of color balance apply to any definition of the picture space whatever its extent and however it is organized—as important in the limited spatial context of a half-length portrait as in the much greater, more open space of a landscape or townscape.

The greater the actual distance you wish to convey, the more alert you have to be to the color cues that make the image work. In a broad landscape where there are dominant colors such as greens or earthy browns you have to examine how these change with distance, and which precise values of tone and color will "pull forward: the foreground plane while "pushing" the distant areas away. Sometimes it is necessary to play up the brilliance of foreground colors, or the tonal emphasis, in order not to lose the diminishing scale of values in the background.

The pictorial arrangement of color also depends upon where you want to place the point of focus in your drawing. If you have an interesting focal area in the middle ground, this has to be "played" in the right key against the foreground and background so that it does not become only an incidental part of the image. You may find that the darker tones defining this area are in the middle range of the tonal scale, and the values used to describe closer objects need to be carefully adapted in their apparent contrasts. The foreground must be treated in a way that establishes its closeness but leads the eye toward the focal point in the middle ground.

VANISHING POINTS

The simplest perspective system is based on a single vanishing point that is set on the horizon line. Parallel horizontal lines going back into space appear to converge on that point but lines or planes that are vertical in your view remain vertical in a drawing. When you face a building corner-on, with the sides of the building receding from you on either side, there will be two sets of receding parallel lines converging on two vanishing points on the horizon line, one the left and one to the right (two-point perspective).

In the first picture, below, the furrows in a plowed field run across our vision, the spaces between them becoming progressively smaller as the field recedes. In the second picture our viewpoint is altered, so that the furrows run away, converging at a vanishing point on the horizon.

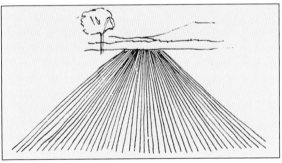

EXPERT TIP

A basic element of perspective drawing is the establishment of a horizon line that corresponds to your eye level. Broadly speaking, horizontal lines above your eye level appear to slant down toward the horizon line, while those below your eye level travel upward.

Light and tone

PENCIL AND WATERCOLOR
by Elisabeth Harden

All types of drawing require an understanding of relative tone and the distinction between tone and shadow. In figure drawing the use of tone is particularly important, for when elaboration is required—for example into a portrait likeness or to describe fur collars or other textures—it is likely that purely linear solutions will prove inadequate.

Tone is dependent upon light; it is in effect the other side of the light area of a solid form. Examine a sphere with one source of light, in other words a stream or flood of light coming from one direction only, and observe through half shut eyes. This method of analyzing tonal

Light is an important element of these three drawings. The same tree was sketched under different kinds of lights in an attempt to develop a free interpretation of the image. The varying approaches to the level of detail, treatment of the foreground mass, and depiction of the color moods give each sketch a distinctly different character, although the subject is recognizably the same.

EXPERT TIP

In the diagram of the sphere, most of the light from above and the left hits the sphere, but some travels on, bounces off a vertical plane and returns to lighten the dark side. The darkest area on the sphere is at the greatest point of turn, and this is a good general rule to be observed. The lighting of the cube, coming from above and left, causes two differing tones on the planes, the one furthest from the light source being the darkest. Shadows help establish the surface on which the cube stands.

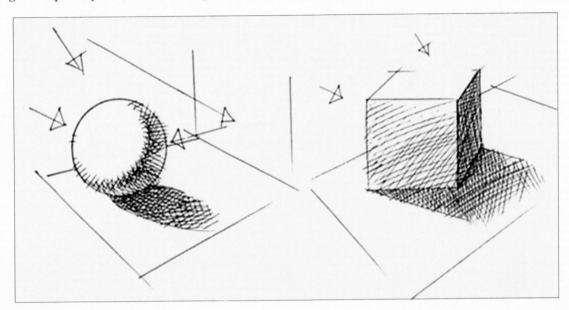

values is very useful, for by narrowing the eyes in this fashion the relationship between darks and lights is heightened; with half tones, mid-grays to light grays for example, it proved essential.

The sphere sits on a flat surface, lit from one side. Apart from the shadow cast from it onto the supporting surface, a full range of tonal contrasts will be apparent within itself, from the area closest to the light source to the darker parts turned furthest away. This is the basis of understanding relative tone and its use in describing solid forms with pencil, chalk, pen, or other drawing implement. A diagram showing the effects of tone can be seen above.

Shadows are the projected shapes of the lighted object onto other surfaces—when understood fully but dangerous if misused or allowed to take over control. It is essential always to be aware of the differences between tone and shadow.

When setting out to draw the spherical form already described, the soft-edged dark tone should be very carefully observed, running as it will around the edge but probably sitting at some distance inside the contour. This is a significant distance and should be measured with great care.

To the outer side of this soft arc of tone is a fillet of lighter tone, not as light as the area of the form in the full glare of the light source but probably approximating to the lighter middle tones between the extremes of light and dark. It is caused by reflection; light strikes the surface of the horizontal support and bounces back onto the underside of the sphere. This is known as reflected light and is a valuable aid to describing full, rounded forms; its position and tone relative both to the contour edge of the solid and the area of the solid in the full flare of light are likely to prove critical.

OUTDOOR SUBJECTS

Outdoor work presents a wealth of
possibilities—landscape and seascape,
parks and gardens, town views, and
without the day-to-day movements of
their inhabitants. The drawbacks of
sketching outdoors, such as they are,
have a lot to do with the
practicalities—how to carry the
materials and equipment you may
need, especially for color work, and
how to protect yourself against the
more extreme weather conditions
without handicapping your sightlines
and your drawing hand.

Portraying atmosphere

When you confront the enormous scope of the world outdoors, you will need to devise some means of focusing your attention. In strange or familiar places, you could fill several sketchbooks standing on one spot, so you have to be selective. As with all subjects, you are dealing with space and form, light and color, but these elements are large and out of your control. Basic considerations are fitting the sketch to your sketchbook page, framing the image effectively, and adapting the visual information to the qualities of your chosen medium. How you approach the work also depends upon whether you are trying to capture a broad view and the general atmosphere, or details such as changing skies and the qualities of light affecting the appearance of landscape or architecture. Fortunately, there will be occasions when you can easily do both, but often your first task is to survey the scene and work out your priorities.

PLANTED PATIO
by Jane Strother

Fluid transitions from bright sunlight to deep shade create the atmosphere of Jane Strother's attractively planted patio (opposite page). She used a deep blue watercolor base for the shadow areas, yellow for the strongest highlights, and merges these two elements through dabs and streaks of watercolor overlaid with colored pencil hatching in middle range of greens, blues, and reds.

EXPERT TIP
Trust your instincts—when you see something immediately arresting, whether a full view or a special detail, sketch your first impression very rapidly. If you have time you can try different viewpoints or approaches, but don't lose the opportunity for a good sketch by being indecisive in the first instance.

ATMOSPHERIC LANDSCAPE
by Tom Robb

Tom Robb contrives an extremely effective atmospheric landscape with bands of color hatched with felt-tip pens. The directional strokes enhance the brooding presence of the heavy sky over the flat landscape.

These next few pages refer to those qualities of an outdoor subject that do not contribute to the basic elements of form and color, which have already been described, but to the sense of time, place, and specific conditions. We spend our days moving between indoor and outdoor locations, absorbing almost instinctively a distinct feeling of the differences between them. These differences exist not only in the simple terms of open or enclosed spaces, but also more subtly—in light, air, vapor, transient effects that move and change within the given frameworks.

It is not always possible to see these things as material colors and textures for which you can find equivalents among your drawing materials. They are insubstantial elements that create the atmosphere of an image, acting upon the solid material qualities of the subject, but their effects can be seen and identified if you train yourself to unravel the different levels of visual information you receive. You will then be a step closer to understanding how to describe them in a drawing.

Because you have, of necessity, to play an interpretive role in capturing these elements, it is

PASTEL ON COLORED PAPER
by John Elliot

Using the long side of a pastel stick rather than the tip creates an atmospheric, grainy texture showing the paper color beneath, and has the practical advantage of covering the surface quickly. Linear details and flashes of brilliant color give a framework to the massed hues.

EXPERT TIP
When painting outdoors make full use of color accents, such as brilliantly colored flowers among trees and grasses, and atmospheric light effects, even when they are only fleetingly seen, to enhance the range of tone and color variation.

particularly helpful to study how other artists have conveyed atmospherics in their color work. Look, for instance, at Cézanne's shimmering, faceted landscapes, Bonnard's colorful, sunlit interiors, Constable's cloud-laden skies, Turner's swirling seastorms, and the Impressionists' grasp of a range of atmospheres as variable as summery riverside scenes and the smoky townscapes of encroaching urbanism. These are, of course, mainly seen in paintings rather than drawings, but the two disciplines always overlap, and if you study the brushwork carefully you will find parallels with drawing techniques. There are also more recent examples of color drawings by contemporary artists that grapple with similarly complex effects of light and color. Sometimes it is by borrowing or adapting another artist's solution that you come upon

EVENING MOOD

This pencil study was started on a late Fall evening and finished later in the studio. The artist exploited the fact that the sun was low on the horizon on the left-hand side, bathing the tower in a pink flow of light and plunging the body of the church into deep shadow. The last of the sun catches the tombstones in the foreground and sets them brilliantly against the dark shadows. With the early moon in the right hand corner, this picture is given an eerie melancholy.

something that is all your own. In any event, learning from others is never wasted, as it complements the direct analysis you apply to your own observations.

Time and season

SPRING
by Elisabeth Harden

Your outdoor sketches may include individual natural subjects and details as well as broader landscape views. Here a plum tree in blossom above a bright mass of flowers provides plenty of visual interest and captures the mood of spring.

Surface effects of color and tonal modeling are influenced by the direction, strength, and color quality of the light falling on them. The quality of natural light changes according to the time of day and season, so if you can capture a particular quality in an outdoor subject, you will add an extra dimension to the sense of location. It is described by the overall color key, the relationships of the areas of light and shade and the individual notes of color provided by highlights and color accents.

You can probably call to mind occasions when you have been struck by a particular quality of illumination on a familiar scene that gives a sudden strange beauty to a normally mundane view. There is a kind of late afternoon light that in the city causes tall buildings to stand out as golden planes against a darkening sky. There is an intense midday effect in high summer when the light is so strong that it almost washes out colors, and there is a harsh, cold light when winter sun reflects off snow. We can call to mind many of these general impressions, especially of extreme conditions, but it is not always easy to define precisely the relative values that create them.

The task of studying such effects to reproduce them in drawing is made more difficult by the fact that they are by nature transient. You cannot sit all day watching the color of afternoon light. You can hope—but not guarantee—that a similar quality will appear for a time on another day. This is an area where acute but rapid observation is needed, where you must train your memory as well as your eyes to take in the color cues and learn to trust your responses to the passing moment. When working on a fully rendered drawing you may have to be dependent on sketches and color notes rather than direct observation.

EXPERT TIP

When working outdoors, interleave your sketchbook pages with sheets of tissue or greaseproof paper. Use the paper as a hand-rest when you are working on a page opposite one that has already been drawn on, to protect the surface and prevent smudging. If you want to move on after completing a sketch and need to close your sketchbook to make it more easily portable, slip tissue between pages where there is color that may not be completely dry, or those on which you have used loose pastel color, so that you do not get an offprint from one page to another or two pages stuck together.

WINTER LANDSCAPE
by John Elliot

In this pastel drawing the dark-colored paper gives a dense, threatening mood to a wintry landscape.

NIGHT LIGHT
by Vincent Milne

It is very difficult to achieve a quality of night light, as the darkness has a paradoxical translucency. Vincent Milne succeeds in reproducing the effect with blended pastel colors, and enhances the effect of dim light in the sky by silhouetting the buildings as hard-edged, solid shapes.

SUMMER
by John Plumb

The artist has made clever use of shape and color to represent clear summer afternoon light creating long, dark shadows. The angle of the cast shadows is one significant element; the color changes in the shadowed details of the hanging plants and swing frame give the image even greater depth and authenticity.

To make these rapid studies, you can for the time being give secondary consideration to form, which will not change and can be studied at more leisure. You need only to sketch out a view roughly to make a "map" on which the color values can be located. If you have a particular subject in mind that you can revisit over a period of time, it might be worthwhile making line sketches that you can photocopy, using the copy sketches as the basis for color notation to save time and allow you to immerse yourself in studying the transient color effects. However you arrange your opportunities to study the subject, there are particular elements to look out for that provide the necessary clues to the qualities you wish to capture.

When you are looking at a subject in which there are large blocks or areas of local color, try to identify the precise color values both in relation to each other and to the source of illumination. In a townscape, for example, a white wall may be washed with a yellow or pink tinge that seems very vivid against a clear blue sky. In landscape, look at the range of greens, their clarity and color bias toward blue or yellow. In the garden, think about the color changes between the solid materials of walls, paths, or fences and the more complex color values of the plants and grass.

It is the tonal scale of a drawing that makes or breaks the sense of illumination, and this must be observed not only in terms of color intensity and light or dark values but also with close attention to edge qualities and gradations of light and shade. Do the shadows that model form show abrupt transitions between light and dark, or a wide range of middle tones? Does the light emphasize contours, creating hard-edged shapes, or soften and merge the forms? Does it etch the textures more strongly, or underplay surface differences? Cast shadows are crucial to a strong lighting effect—do these have heavy tonal density and solid outlines or a more fluid, amorphous presence? What is their direction and extent in relation to the light source?

At the same time be alert to the color qualities in the shadows as these will later help to give surface activity to the color rendering. Look for dark tints of blue, green, purple, or red in shadows, as these provide color cues that can be played off against the lighter tones. Note also which shadows are in fact neutral in color value, but for this very reason have the effect of of intensifying the pure hues and pale tones. Finally, look for the color accents—not of local color, but of reflected colors and highlights. Under certain lights, these may reflect an intense pink or gold, or perhaps cold bluish tones. Compare the depth of reflected color according to the surface quality— whether there are distinct patches of solid color subtle passing tints.

SHADOWS

Shadow patterns are described in different ways in these drawings, in one by distinct color changes, in the other by tonal scale. Cast shadows on the ground form linear patterns in the bottom two drawings, and both have been treated with a tonal range of emphatic contrast.

OUTDOOR SUBJECTS

81

Time and season

Exterior light

When you seek to capture an effect of natural light, it is not usually possible to obtain all the information you need in a single period of concentrated drawing. Rather, you must train your eye to be alert to the cues of color, tonal contrast, and patterns of light and shade that are typical of a particular time and place. If you make a number of rapid studies of a whole view or individual details, you build a body of reference work that subsequently can be used as the basis for constructing more complex and detailed drawings. At the same time, this process gives further opportunity to develop your visual and technical skills.

The main color study in this sequence of drawings shows a garden view in afternoon light, with rich, strong colors under full sun and hard-edged dark shadows cast from the standing objects. In the two smaller drawings of the pot plants, the artist investigates the different qualities of cool morning light, with pale tints and cool shadows, and the more intense light of evening in which the colors are all tinged with red and cold.

The smaller studies go into further detail of shadow patterns and color values, trying out varied techniques of watercolor and colored pencil drawing. You should always bear in mind how the medium and technique that you select can most aptly convey the qualities of your subject.

Composing a landscape

A convenient way to start drawing a landscape is to view the landscape through a viewing frame; this certainly helps to choose the best pictorial composition. For the beginner the frame is an essential piece of equipment. It is not absolutely vital to have a folding easel or a stool, but if a study is going to be made to a near-finished state outside it can be very tiring to stand in one placing holding a sketchbook.

Start by drawing a rectangle on your paper. This is to represent the picture plane as seen through the viewing frame. Decide where you are going to start, and with a 4B pencil make a continuous line drawing of the scene in front of you that you have selected through your viewing frame, going around the main outline of all the features.

Do not at this stage get involved in any detail because that could interfere with the overall structure and composition of the drawing. Once all the large features are drawn, add lines designating all the large areas that are in shadow. If you intend to use the drawing as a basis for a watercolor, you will probably have sufficient information for it at this stage.

USING A FRAME

Use of a frame can be of great advantage both in landscape and townscape drawing as a device for finding interesting angles of composition. The examples on the right show the same landscape through three different viewing frames.

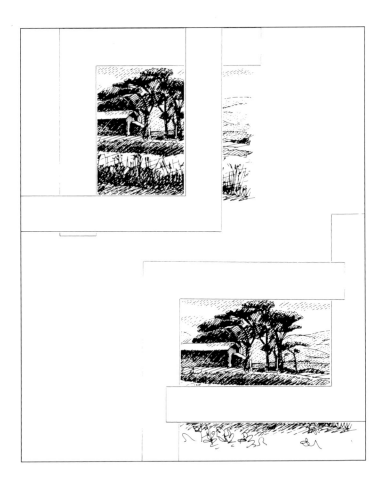

PICTURE PLANE

You can see that by altering the position of the picture plane the composition of this painting is altered. In photography every time you point your camera in a slightly different direction at the same landscape you are altering the camera's picture plane and you will therefore take a different photograph. The artist's eye, when working in a representational manner, is reacting to the landscape in a similar way to the camera. The simplest frame (left) will help you to decide upon the most stimulating picture plane for any scene.

Composing a landscape

If, however, you intend to take the drawing to the state of a finished work there and then, starting working greater detail into areas in the middle ground, so that the drawing begins to develop a sense of three-dimensional space.

Now start to outline the areas that are in deeper shadow within the already drawn area of shadow. Shade both these areas again. Now concentrate in greater detail on those areas of the composition that you have decided to make the focal point. If the focal point of your composition is in the middle distance, again, do not over-embellish. Successful drawings may depend far more on what is suggested to be there than what actually is. Always leave room in your composition for the imagination of the viewer. If the drawing is overdetailed, the viewer is not encouraged to do more than scan, for all the information that is required for the viewer to understand what he or she is looking at is immediately apparent. If the middle ground is overdeveloped, it also makes it impossible to do anything with finer-detailed work on the immediate foreground.

To attempt to bring the whole composition to a high degree of finish, as many beginners do, may result in the drawing just looking incredibly flat and cluttered with too much visual information, so that it may even become difficult to see the overall intention of your original concept. Remember that your mind perceives far more detail than is physically possible to record in your drawing. Select those elements of the composition that are visually most useful to you.

LANDSCAPE
by Jane Strother

To capture the character of a landscape it is often necessary to use the color cues of the natural model as a basic register that the artist can manipulate in terms of color interactions. Jane Strother picks out the contrast of yellows and warm browns against cold blues and purples in this open, windswept view.

LANDSCAPES IN CHARCOAL

Charcoal has many advantages for the beginner. Large areas of tone can be put in very rapidly, and the intensity can be varied by rubbing, blowing, or brushing etc. If you want to alter the form—i.e. shape—it can be easily done, moreover, with a soft putty eraser. The richness of tone achievable with charcoal is immense, from the palest grays to the blackest of blacks, and with the addition of white chalk and a putty eraser to bring out highlights, charcoal as a medium can be fully utilized.

There are, however, two distinct disadvantages to charcoal when working out of doors. It is not unknown to have a drawing in an advanced state

SAPLINGS IN CHARCOAL
by T. H. Saunders

This stand of young saplings was rendered in charcoal and white chalk. The chalk has been used predominantly in the foliage and gives the impression of flickering light passing through the leaves.

when a sudden gust of wind removes half your hard-won image before you have had time to apply a fixative. It is also quite a dirty medium. However, it is the vulnerability of the work while in progress that sometimes makes this an unsuitable medium for working outdoors.

Vacations

The prospect of having time off, whether a day or two of leisure of a lengthy trip to an exotic location, has a dual purpose for the dedicated sketcher. Here a new subjects and interests, a sense of color and energy, unfamiliar places, and different ways people behave when they are relaxing and enjoying life without the need to keep up appearances or watch the clock. And here is the time and opportunity that the artist needs to be able to sketch freely and with a fresh eye, as both a participant in and an observer of the scene.

There are different kinds of holiday sketches, some being the kind of reportage that you might practice anywhere, the difference being that your clear intention is to record a subject because it is unusual or unfamiliar to you. Ancient and impressive cities, hilltop villages, street markets, docks, waterside cafés—all these interesting locations exist in countries all around the world. You may pay greater attention to them when you are on holiday either because they are distinctly different and more picturesque than the sights in your own locale, or simply because you have more time to view such things objectively. The formal and pictorial interests—structures, composition, color, detail—are fundamentally similar whatever the subject or location. Alternatively, it may be less the objective image of the scene or view that interests you, more the mood or atmosphere that sums of the flavor of life and leisure in an unfamiliar place. And there are individual themes that may take your attention—the beach, for example, might be regarded as a colorful and informal life class for study of the human figure.

SEASCAPE

This seascape with rocks has been drawn in pastel pencil, which is much harder to master than the conventional pastel stick, but allows great control over your drawing. Pastel pencils do not blend together quite so easily, but they are an ideal medium to use outdoors.

FELT-TIP AND MARKER

This series of images is designed to describe the idea rather than the reality of vacations, taking in different aspects of the events and locations that might be encountered on a vacation trip. Each image is based on something seen, but the references come from a variety of sources and the individual sketches have almost a collaged effect. They are worked very quickly and loosely with bold, simple materials. The bright colors are intended to bring to mind the visual qualities of holiday postcards.

EXPERT TIP

Think about the types of materials you will need to pack with your holiday luggage. If you are gong to somewhere particularly exotic, you will obviously want the capability to sketch in color. Take a watercolor box and pastels or crayons, together with monochrome media. Consider what is the largest size of sketchbook you might want to use, and that you can conveniently pack and travel with. Keep materials and equipment to the minimum, but try not to restrict your technical options too much.

The harbor

Building up layers of pigment gradually the artist has created a work based on his careful observation of colors and their patterns—rather than objects and their colors. He sees around the the boats and blocks in the background, he sees into the boats and colors their depths, he sees highlights and burnishes in around them. Above all the the image is a vision of shapes with color that, when completed, suggest colors with form. Unhampered by line the artist's colors live with a structure of their own.

1 *The artist saw this harbor scene as a series of color patches and shapes. In his sketch, above, he first worked out the skeleton of the composition in lines of French gray and then noted down briefly the relationship of the colors and their forms.*

2 *The shapes of the boats and the surrounding landscape have been worked up as areas of flat tone with strong directional lines. Each color has been related to its neighbor and has been used as a foundation from which to build up further layers of color. The pink of the b luff in the background echoes the pink-purple of the boat on the right of the picture.*

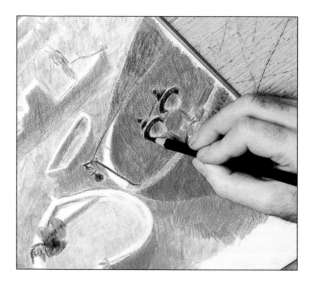

3 *Working systematically from the front to the back of the drawing, details emerge slowly, as color boundaries are established. Here, black is used to draw in the boat lights as a positive focal point—one of the few sharp details in this generally soft color treatment.*

4 *The background and horizon have been kept very soft and misty purposely to emphasize distance—sharper detail would have pulled them forward too far. Both the colors and the forms fade in a muted haze as they would in reality.*

5 *The artist has used his knowledge of color very cleverly to draw our pattern, using the negative and positive elements of the forms. For example, he has left the paper white on the rims of the boats to produce a pattern of curved outlines against the inside of the boats, which have been left as flat areas without shadow or color depth.*

Plantation

Using a system of carefully placed areas of cross-hatching the artist has created a very positive color statement, integral with a structural style. Color grids have been applied one over another to create areas of texture and tone. Overlapping hues have produced very complex color mixtures that stand out against the white background like shadows on a wall—blue behind yellow, red behind green. The directional nature of the lines creates both static forms in the trees that rise in serried rows from the plain, and moving texture in the sky where wispy clouds float over the distant peaks.

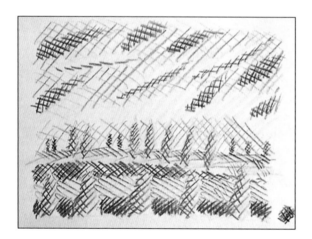

1 *In this preliminary sketch of a cypress plantation, the artist quickly established the colors he will use for the final drawing, and the way he has laid down the color suggests the style and treatment he should use in it. From this point it becomes almost a mechanical exercise to produce the finished image.*

2 *The first stage is hatched in on the paper in blue, leaving areas white where the colors are not intended to mix with the blue. The blue pencil has been used with varying pressure to create light and dense lines. The way it has been sharpened has allowed thick and finely hatched grids to develop, which gives the image depth.*

EXPERT TIP:
HATCHING WITH PASTEL
Draw clear, roughly parallel, closely spaced lines. Fix pastel color before applying another layer, then work a second color into the first.

3 *Yellow lines were laid across the foreground and in the white areas to convey the warmth of the evening light. Long, straight yellow lines drawn across the sky lend a still quality to the sky, at the same time highlighting its expanse.*

4 *This close-up shows how cross-hatching with different colors creates an optical mixing of color. Red applied over blue creates a purple, red hatched across yellow produces an orange, and blue over yellow creates green. By overlapping grids at different angles great depth of color is achieved. Straight lines have been used for the background to contrast with the slightly curved strokes on the cypresses that exaggerate the rounded form of these trees.*

5 *In the completed drawing, above, the many lines and few applied colors combine to form a cohesive whole. The dense build-up of lines in the middle distance forms a solid base against which snowy white peaks of the horizon and the white edges of the cypress trees are highlighted. It also provides a visual mid-point in the composition.*

Eiffel tower

The artist has created a very confident, cool, and controlled study of this famous landmark. Despite the hazy monotone effects in this work it does in fact hide a wealth of color. Gradations in hue take the eye from the foreground along the distant perspective of the tree-lined boulevard to a focal point, where, at the end of a receding row of dark trees, we are over-shadowed by the tense span of the structure's feet. Like a dinosaur it towers above with its head in the clouds. We do not see the top, it is out of the composition, there by inference only, just as the color is hinted at—black against white, negative against positive.

1 *Having worked up the sky with a loose hatching of sky blue the artist concentrates on developing the central features of the drawing, choosing to work from the focal point outward, right. The dark gray silhouette of the tower stands starkly against the paler sky.*

2 *The dominating perspective is developed by drawing in shapes on either side of the avenue that leads the eye to the tower, below. The artist is also trying to show that lighter colors, such as blue and lilac, recede whereas dark colors come forward and thus exaggerate perspective.*

3 *The highly stylized bushes beneath the tower create a balance, echoing the shape of the tower, left. Their dark closely worked forms, produced with heavy pencil pressure of indigo over sap green, stand proud of the loose, lighter background and create a weight in the image that takes the eye down from the towering shadow very firmly to the solid ground below.*

4 *Using the edge of a ruler, the artist achieves a mechanical precision in representing the manicured edge of the boulevard's grass verge. It can be helpful to use straight edges to mask an area of coloring temporarily, to allow the strokes to be drawn freely without worrying that they will end outside the edge desired. The pencil used was sharpened to expose a considerable length of lead, allowing the artist to use rapid, broad strokes to cover a relatively large area with speed.*

6 *To soften the linear nature of the pencil strokes on the medium-grain paper, a plastic eraser has been used to create a smooth fine color where the light is so bright that only a hint of tone is needed. Halfway through the drawing the artist sprays on some fixative to prevent the color from smudging.*

5 *The very distinct areas of light and shade produce negative and positive forms. Here, color is applied with small, delicate strokes that allow the paper to show through, and achieve a very pale tonal gradation through pressure rather than by color mixing.*

7 *The color is seen clearly here, below, as areas of shape, textured by the pressure of the application and the direction of the strokes. Very slight changes in the flow of the lines are visible in the base of the tower, the trees and the shaped bushes.*

8 *A geometric organization becomes quite apparent in the finished image. The shape of the dark area of trees on the right mirrors that of the area of grass on the left. Similarly the lit area beneath the trees on the right mirrors the segment of middle distance trees on the left. The triangles of the cypress trees emulate the triangle of the tower. All the lines converge at the right foot of the arch. Pressure, used cleverly with color, relieve this almost monochromatic image by increasing its tonal variety.*

Garden scene

When practicing landscape drawing it is often unnecessary to travel far to find appropriate subjects. Your local park or, in this case, your own garden can provide plenty of interest and variety. The strong, dark shapes of the yew trees contrast with the bright, delicate flowers.

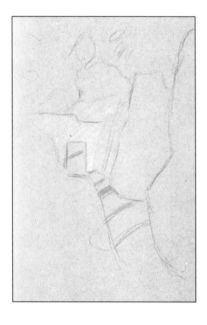

1 *Lightly draw in the general composition, paying particular attention to the yew trees that are the strongest forms, and to their shadows.*

2 *Block in the masses by building up layers of hatching, using an underlying Naples yellow or Cream for the yews to provide a light surface other than that of the paper itself.*

3 *Continue to build the color and shape of the yews, overlapping various colors—a bluish green, a bright dark green, Purple, Burnt Sienna, Vermillion red.*

4 *Put in cross-hatching to build up color until the final effect is achieved.*

5 *Work more detail into the background and into the middle area of the drawing, adding definition to the flower bed on the left using Orange, Crimson lake, and Yellow.*

6 *Put in a dark background—Tuscan red, Black, Real green, Peacock green, a red, and Buttermilk to lighten real darks. Balance back and foreground shapes.*

7 *In this exercise, use a technique of hatching and cross-hatching to buid up several layers of color. Test the effect of a dark background by cutting out a piece of dark paper of an approximately similar shape and holding it in the appropriate area.*

Sky studies

Make at least three drawings of skies. You can either work outside or from a window. You will have to look out for particular days and times of day that will be best for drawing—those when you will be able to see the most dramatic effects. Rain or an approaching storm, sunset or sunrise can offer very different drawing approaches.

As well as recreating the mood of the weather in your drawing, your main problem is going to be drawing movement. Clouds move quickly,

light changes constantly, nothing in nature stays still. Just as you will need to look intently, memorize what you see and record it quickly. Before you start, give some thought to which drawing medium or media you are going to use. You will probably find that a tonal or color medium such as ink wash, charcoal, or pastel will give you the most scope, and that pencils and pens are less useful.

1 *This drawing gives a good impression of both depth and movement, with the black conté crayon used in gentle criss-crossing curves.*

2 *Wind clouds can make dramatic swirling patterns, which can be exaggerated for effect, as in this pastel drawing.*

3 *Notice the depth in this conté drawing. Skies are not flat; they are subject to the laws of perspective, and clouds become smaller as they approach the horizon.*

4 *The emphasis in this pastel drawing is on the pattern in the sky, but the way the white pastel has been applied suggests movement.*

Pastel landscapes

Just like ordinary pastels, oil pastels can be mixed on the paper by overlaying. They can't be blended by rubbing, but the color can be melted with turpentine or white spirit, so that you can mix them on the paper very much as you would mix paints on a palette.

The other great virtue of oil pastels is they don't need fixing, and you can build up layers of color without worrying about the top layer falling off. A disadvantage is that in hot weather they tend to melt even without the aid of turpentine, becoming both messy to use and difficult to handle.

1 *The dark color is spread with a rag dipped in white spirit.*

2 *A brush, similarly dipped in white spirit, is now used to spread the color in the sky areas.*

3 *The artist now draws over the spread color with the tip of the pastel stick, introducing a more linear element into the foreground of the landscape.*

4 *This method, which combines drawing and painting, is a very quick and effective way of building up areas of color, ideal for location work when time is often limited.*

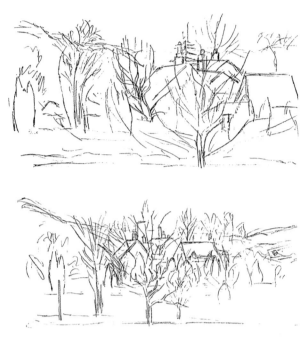

1 *The artist, Rosalind Cuthbert, has worked out the basic composition in the first two sketches (above left), and then made further studies of the shapes of the trees beside the house, an important feature in the finished drawing.*

2 *The final drawing has been made in pastel, using the sketches and color notes as references. The drawing's center of interest is the house with the line of trees in front, so the artist has treated the central foreground tree very lightly and delicately, so that it does not form a "block" for the eye.*

Beach boys

Taking a color snapshot as a reference the artist has analyzed the subject and decided to depict the scene in more sympathetic tones—in very pale, bleached colors reminiscent of bright sunlight on a hot day by the sea. The camera cannot "quote" what was actually seen, so here the artist is giving back life and emotion to a picture that has been "flattened." Using transfer paper, a brief but accurate guideline was drawn onto the paper and patches of reference colors were then added over the whole area. Very gentle strokes of pale pigments were then applied overall, particularly in and around the two figures. The artist took care to leave large areas of highlight and graded the tones very subtly into neatly defined areas of shade.

1 *After sketching in an outline for the figures, the artist has roughed in areas of color using very delicate masses of line and tone.*

2 *Since all the colors are intended to be pale it is important to maintain a very gentle touch with the pencil. The pigment quite clearly sits on the surface texture of the paper— too much pressure and too heavy a color would be deposited.*

3 *The completed drawing shows just how much color can be created and maintained within a very narrow tonal band. The secret of its success is the very considered delicate handling of the pencils. Note how a smooth uptake of mixed pigment is used for the flesh tones in comparison with the background where more demonstrative strokes and linework combine in the rocks and seaweed. At the first glance, this sun-bleached scene belies the wealth of color it actually contains.*

Gallery

LANDSCAPE (RIGHT)
by Olwen Tarrant

Olwen Tarrant brings out the pure colors in the landscape, enhancing the balance of hues and tones to create a vividly descriptive composition. The drawing is worked in pastel on a heavily-grained, dark-toned paper. The artist develops form and texture by varying the pastel strokes, in some areas building dense masses of color, in others exploiting the linear qualities of the medium. Where the grain of the paper creates an effect of broken color, the brighter hues are intensified by the contrast with the underlying dark tone.

TALL PALMS
by Ashley Potter

This oil pastel drawing of tall palms plays sunshine yellows and citrus greens against clear blues and mauves to produce a vibrant effect. this drawing was the basis for a silkscreen print, in which a more formal design was schemed with brilliant color.

Buildings and townscapes

All the theories and pictorial attitudes that have already been discussed in this section apply equally well to the study of Townscapes and Buildings. It is possible to make a very successful drawing of landscape where no buildings at all are present, but the inclusion of buildings adds a further pictorial element which can be used to great effect. The geometrical precision of buildings, when used in contrast to natural landscape, can create a visual tension and the same is equally true in reverse of a row of trees lining a central city street, which add an organic

PUBLIC HOUSE

A pencil study of a public house depicting the building in a clear and concise manner. No attempt has been made to include people on what would normally be a busy thoroughfare. The subject of this drawing is categorically the building.

contrast to the geometrical hardness of the adjacent buildings.

For the beginner who wishes to seriously tackle the subject of townscape it is essential to approach the city with an open eye and an open mind. It is not necessary to live in a great metropolis or city renowned for its architectural beauty. Any town or small industrial center canna provide a lifetime of subject matter for the sensitive observer, and even the uniformity of many suburban streets can present a pictorial rhythm unique to the local environment. A row of identical suburban villas might not seem a likely subject, but if the artist concentrates on those details that the owners have added to their homes to give individuality to what were originally identical structures, an interesting drawing can be made of what might otherwise have been dismissed as a mundane and commonplace subject.

Our own contemporary environment presents just as many possibilities. Brightly colored motorcars stacked in rows in a drab concrete

TOWNSCAPES
by Ian Simpson

Two complex "bird's-eye" view townscapes by Ian Simpson, which combine to form a continuous image, depend on a strong graphic framework of ink and pencil line drawing. Within this structure, color washes are applied as representational color describing roofs, walls, chimneys, and the street below, enhancing the sense of place and time. Loose brushwork adds to the detail of the images, suggesting a range of surface qualities.

multistorey car park could quite easily be turned into an interesting pictorial study. The grotesque silhouette of an industrial plant, which obeys none of the proportions necessary in an inhabited building, can give the artist a whole range of visual possibilities: such structures obey their own strong logic governed by the industrial processes they are designed to serve.

Another area of townscape that is well worth investigation if the forest of billboards and fluorescent displays that give any shopping precinct its great visual variety of shapes and colors. The city at night can be particularly visually exciting, its multitude of light sources casting shadows in all directions. A good beginning for a work done at night might be a gas station, with its constant movement and brightly lit forecourt, representing an oasis of light and color in an otherwise dimly-lit suburban street.

For those of you who wish to represent the townscape in a less impressionistic manner, a working knowledge of perspective is very useful. But because few streets are build dead straight or uniformly, simple, two-point perspective is

THE MONASTERY OF MAR SABA
by David Bomberg

This chalk and oil pastel sketch conjures a vivid sense of place from lines and streaks of bright color on a warm brown background. Fine draftsmanship is evident in both the structure of the composition and the sensitivity of line.

THAMES BARRIER, LONDON

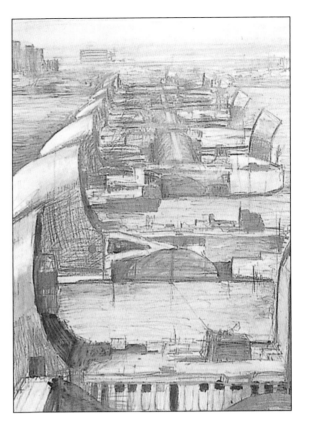

111

In these two pen and wash drawings of the Thames Barrier in London, an optimistic, vibrant view of man's achievement in the urban environment is presented. A putty eraser has been used extensively to lift the light areas.

essentially too limiting and an understanding of the laws of multi-vanishing point perspective is more useful. However, it is not necessary to study perspective independently of undergoing the experience of actually drawing. If the pictorial basics of good observation and the picture-plane are clearly understood, an exciting rendition of a townscape can be successfully completed with the minimum of perspective knowledge.

Take any street scene and view it as you would a landscape, through a viewing frame. Draw a picture-plane on your paper. Now draw a contin-uous line corresponding first of all to the overall silhouette of the major buildings nearest to you. Try to avoid seeing each building individually. See the whole street as a continuous shape that is divided into individual buildings by the addi-

ONE-POINT PERSPECTIVE

In one-point perspective only two faces of the cube are visible. One side is seen straight on, and there is only one vanishing point.

VANISHING POINTS

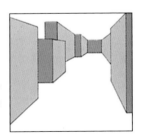

Vanishing points are located on the horizon line. However, they will often be obscured by buildings or other objects. When this occurs, it is nevertheless crucial to know where the vanishing would be located. Although the converging lines will not

reach their ultimate destinations, only by locating their vanishing points will you be able to judge the correct angles.

tion of the features that make each building separate from its neighbor. Observe how a large building at the end of the street appears smaller than a more modest building nearer to you, and how a relatively close traffic sign can obscure your view of even the largest buildings. Again the main problem is in believing what you see and having the confidence to record it.

The visual possibilities of townscape are very broad, from a large panoramic view of the city drawn from a high vantage-point, to a closely observed view through the half-open gates of a factory yard.

The first attempt for those who do not have easy access to a town could well be to portray a local church. This is a much-worked subject for beginners . . . and many of the resultant drawings are quite uninteresting because the drawing is carried out in purely topographical terms. But

there are other ways in which to tackle such drawings, and indeed with imagination this type of subject has many possibilities. Street scenes of villages and small towns have considerable visual potential. Corner shops, squares and market places, statues and war memorials, all hold great pictorial value. Again it is often the contrasts of architectural periods in buildings and their proximity to contemporary construc-

TOWNSCAPE SKETCH
by Ian Ribbons

This quick sketch is a good example of including people in your drawing without going into too much detail. The artist has used active dashed and dotted ink line to suggest the mood, with pale washes of yellow and neutral colors laid in to convey the flat façades of the sunlit buildings.

PENCIL SKETCH

*This pencil study is a good example of multi-point perspective.
All the elements make for complication; the rising steps on one
side and the lane moving away downhill on the other, and the
fact that none of the buildings are square to one another, make
it very difficult for the beginner to work out all the various
vanishing points. The viewing frame should be used to
understand the relationship of all the elements.*

tions that can give an interesting visual twist to a contemporary scene.

For those of you with a little more confidence, the inclusion of people in your town or village scene can add another dimension. There is no need to be a master of anatomical drawing to include figures in this type of work. Take a look at the range of human personality that Lowry was able to express with the minimum of detail. Once again it is sharp observation of human character that is all-important to give a beginner the confidence to include figures in his or her drawing.

As in drawing a landscape, try not to ignore those that you might feel to be an intrusion of modern life on the town, such as traffic signals and signs, refuse containers etc. You might not like them, but they are indispensable pictorially. Many beginners omit these things from their drawings in an attempt to portray a street scene

of predominantly older buildings, as though the drawing was done when the buildings were first erected, say the 19th century. Works carried out in this frame of mind inevitably look unconvincing because many other pictorial elements that would have been present in the 19th century are not there—particularly horses and carts, and figures in period costume. Try to see the view in front of you in terms of its pictorial value in a specifically contemporary sense.

USING A SKETCHBOOK

Because of the difficulty of trying to set up an easel and stool in a busy shopping street, the usefulness of a sketchbook comes into its own when drawing buildings or townscapes.

Artists have different ideas about working from sketchbook notes but a useful approach is to think of your sketchbook as a visual diary in which on a day-to-day basis you record those things that are visually stimulating, gathering as much visual information in your quick drawings as possible. Beginners often get the wrong impression about what a sketchbook is for, and fill it with ill-conceived and rather scribbled drawings that two days after they have been done are visually unreadable and carry insufficient information to be of any real value in the studio.

BRIGHTON PIER, ENGLAND

Washes of watercolor and gouache establish distance, atmosphere, and local color in this drawing but the impression of detail and texture is dependent on work with pencil and pen and ink. The strong vertical that divides the picture plane in the foreground is the focal point from which the other elements recede toward the horizon line. Different linear qualities are achieved by drawing with ink over both wet and dry paint so that in some places the line is crisp and precise while elsewhere it diffuses gently into lighter tones.

The sketchbook should be considered the training-ground for quick, accurate drawings in which every line and every mark conveys the maximum of visual information. It is better to record one small detail well than to plaster a page full of arbitrary marks that may mean something to you in the heat of the moment, but which in hindsight convey too loose an impression. The real function of a sketchbook is to record accurate visual information that can be useful in the studio.

As an exercise, try making a drawing from a series of sketches and notes done in one location. When you start to draw your townscape in the studio from your sketches, you will soon discover the sort of information that you should have recorded. Go again to the same location and make some more sketches. In this practical way you will soon understand what you need to record for the sketches to be of any real value. It is particularly when drawing a townscape that the sketchbook is most useful. Obviously, not all finished townscape drawings have to be a composite work from a sketchbook; many works can be finished on location. A more positive approach is thus required for townscape drawing than is required for the more lonely activity of drawing in the countryside.

Special events

Certain events and locations are of special interest for sketching because they are unique or unusual in your experience. These include places that have a particular function and atmosphere, such as a courtroom or theater, and one-off events such as a wedding or public celebration that claim attention for their temporary but important status in the scheme of things. With some of these subjects, it is in their nature that the opportunity to make sketches is relatively restricted by comparison with other everyday situations. You may have limited time, a restricted viewpoint, or you ma be a participant in the event rather than an observer of it, and therefore unable to stand back and take a detached perspective.

In these cases you may reap the benefits of a habit of sketching, given that long-term practice of taking quick but significant visual notes will have sharpened your observation and your ability to record what you see discreetly but in a way that can be useful to you as an artist. Usually your technical means must be kept simple and you can work only with a small sketchbook and a pencil or ballpoint. The quickest way to get an impression of a scene is in a line drawing, but you may wish to add tonal values to give the sketch more atmosphere, and you might also want to make color notes in writing.

The character of your sketch work also depends upon what you wish to achieve from the

WEDDING IN PENCIL AND WATERCOLOR
by Elisabeth Harden

This image was made in preparation for a lithographic print, working out the tone and color balance. The artist's initial ideas came from the event itself, but because of the difficulty of sketching on the spot, the wedding video was used as back-up reference for the sketches. The detail of the flower arrangement was taken from still photographs.

experience. If the function of the sketches is as a simple record of particular aspects of the event, or if you are purely engaged with the immediate visual interest, you can keep your methods equally simple and view the sketches as mainly an interesting document of an unusual occurrence. However, you may alternatively be gathering material for further work, such as a painting or print depicting both the detail and atmosphere of the situation.

REGATTA
by Jake Sutton

This colorful regatta actually contains relatively few colors. The effect comes from the strong values of primary and secondary hues—red, blue, yellow, orange, green—applied in translucent watercolor over the initial drawing. It captures the atmosphere and excitement of the day and the detail of the line of bright flags is a clever touch.

Alhambra gardens

The artist was inspired by the earthenware-pink roof tiles and the reflective pale stucco of the plastered walls in this beautiful garden. She deliberately chose pink tinted paper as a background to this study to echo the pink hues. A colored ground not only alters the effect of the colors applied, because it shines through the translucent pigment, but it also acts as a unifying force throughout the drawing, pulling together all the elements and creating the feeling of a pink light that permeates the image. The white highlights are laid separately and are slowly worked into the blue-grays of the plastered walls. The artist substantiates the pink light by treating the buildings and the foliage separately, maintaining a tight control over the show-through in each area and leaving the viewer in the cool gray shadows with a beautiful view of a warm, pink world beyond.

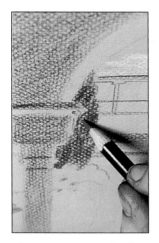

1 *On pink tinted paper the artist first roughs in the basic shapes and areas of her composition as both a compositional and tonal guideline. These colors will form an almost monotone background to the brightness of the sunlit garden.*

2 *White is laid over the highlight areas and contrasts strongly with the deep blue shadows, conveying the brilliance of the sunshine. Where the white is used with the blue, gentle tonal gradations are created.*

3 *A framework of shadow and light is developed, in which the focal points and the basic perspective are sketched. The simple shapes and colors emphasize the positive and negative elements of the image.*

4 *Dark blue and yellow basic leaf shapes are crayoned in, to be mixed with various shades of green later. The blue will darken the green in areas and the yellow will give the impression of light-struck leaves, enlivening the foliage.*

5 *Having drawn in the colored foliage, shadows are reworked in deep hues to give the leaves and flowers dimension and form.*

6 *The final drawing successfully combines restrained color and the exaggerated effects of light. The pink of the paper is carried through in the terracotta tiles, and the dappled shadows across the path in the foreground, and contrasts with the bleaching effect of the harsh light. Once the style of treating highlights and shadows has been decided upon the work developed as a series of patterns of dark and light areas and is quite systematic in its approach.*

Urban landscape

The uncompromising lines of modern offices may not have occurred to you as an obvious subject for a landscape painting or drawing. Here the artist was attracted by the regular geometric lines of the building and has counterpointed these with the brick wall in the foreground. While the drawing is a faithful representation of the subject, the artist has deliberately stressed the strong parallels and, the repeated rectangles of the building's wall and the squares of the windows. At the same time, he has taken a viewpoint that eliminates most of the surrounding cityscape with its softer forms and trees that relieve the harshness and has played down those aspects of landscape that do intrude.

The artist worked very quickly, anxious to establish the broad areas of the drawing. He used colored pencils and lead pencils, handling them loosely and freely in order to get down as much information as possible in the short time available.

This is typical of the sort of information you should collect and the way you should use your sketchbook. It is an important part of your life and should always be with you. It is a diary of your day-to-day activities, a file of information, of details of architecture, for example, of light effects, of people and poses. It should be used every day. In this way you will improve your perceptive powers, your visual memory and your drawing skills.

COLORS USED IN THIS DRAWING

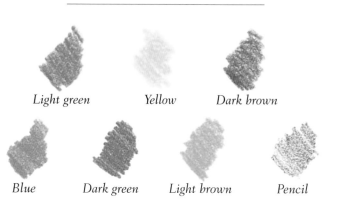

Light green   *Yellow*   *Dark brown*

Blue   *Dark green*   *Light brown*   *Pencil*

1 *The artist records everyday events, makes notes of subjects that interest him, evolves ideas and solves problems in his sketchbook. Here he addresses himself to a subject that might easily be overlooked but that is important to all city dwellers.*

2 *The artist works in pencil, drawing what he sees but simplifying the forms so that the can record his impressions quickly but accurately. He was attracted by the strong verticals and horizontals and he makes these a feature of the sketch.*

3 *He uses a few colored pencils to record local color. This will be useful if he should decide to use this subject in a painting.*

4 *He applies the color with freely handled parallel strokes. In the final picture on page 120 blue has been scribbled into the sky, and this time the color is laid on much more loosely with strokes that vary in direction.*

EXPERT TIP

The overall view – look for surface interest and unusual angles. Bird's eye and worm's eye views of buildings give a very different impression from a frontal, ground level view. Brickwork, ironwork, and interesting structural details of doors, windows, balconies, moldings, etc. are all elements that can be selectively introduced to enliven the basic forms.

PROJECT 10 Battersea power station, London

The scene of angry workers in front of the power station conjures up an image reminiscent of factory workers and urban industrialization at the turn of the century. The artist has deliberately chosen a style that, in its human scale, its handling, color, and its imagery, emulates that of the Futurists who were painting rather similar subject matter in the early 1900s, glorifying the power of industry.

The artist has worked in a systematic fashion using a fine outline to delineate areas of color, and has built up patches of basic lines as a foundation to the heavier layers of color required later. He constantly used a white pencil in order to burnish highlights, such as the sheen on the workers' clothing. Exploring these effects further a typist's stencil was used as a template for burnishing color with an eraser.

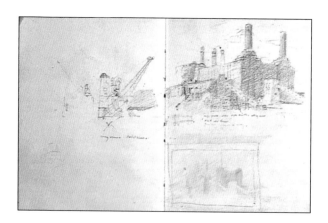

1 *A couple of small pencil sketches, made during an evening walk, suggest an idea to the artist for a composition in color, inspired by the red brick monolith.*

2 *Having masked off the areas of the image with masking tape, the artist sketches in the main elements with a graphite pencil and now begins to add soft base color.*

3 *Laying color quite heavily over the garments of the men at the foot of the drawing, the artist develops strong shapes and a visual story. Using a white pencil the pigment is burnished into highlight areas to create a glossy sheen on the folds of fabric and give a strong stylistic approach to the treatment of color.*

4 *All the main areas of color are blocked in to form a foundation for deeper colors to be worked into for the shadow areas, and white for the areas of highlight.*

5 *Shadows are worked up from the areas of deepest color as here, the artist works black into the edges of dark brown shadows.*

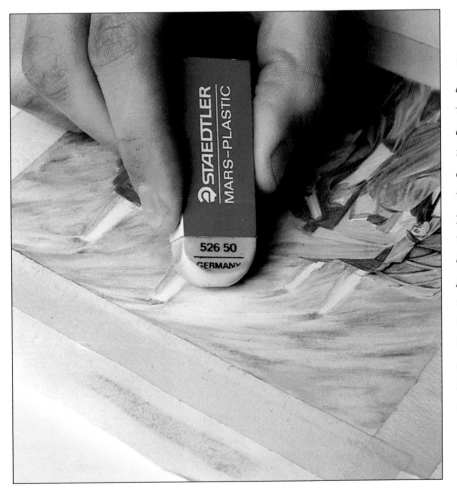

6 *Soft greens, yellows, and oranges were laid with upward strokes across the area of the sky to emulate the movement of smoke. These are then worked over with a plastic eraser, the movements following the direction of the pigment, gradually smoothing, mixing, and burnishing the colors into the background. The smooth effect given by the eraser aptly conveys the sensation of wispy smoke.*

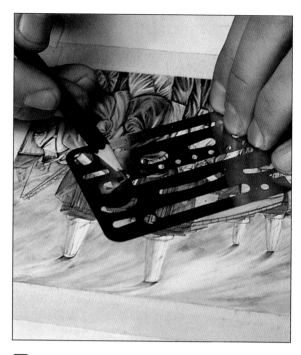

7 To enable the artist to lay color into small areas with greater accuracy and with relatively sharp definition, a typist's stencil was used as a template. He then fixed the drawing with fixative.

8 Once the fixative had dried, where color had become almost too heavy, areas of compacted pigment were scratched away with a designer's knife, used very delicately. This technique gives the colors a wonderful translucence.

EXPERT TIPS

Architectural details—whether or not you have drawn a full view, sometimes it is a particular detail that catches your eye rather than the full building. Quick reference sketches of unusually shaped or colorful features will provide good source material for later, more elaborate works. These are often obvious when you are in a strange place, where everything seems new and fascinating, but if you search more keenly in familiar locations you will see many interesting things that you have previously missed.

Contrasts—most towns and cities are a mixture of old and new architecture, and have planted areas of trees or flowers contrasting with the inorganic nature of the buildings. You have also the option in a street scene to include the movement of people or traffic against the solid structures of the buildings.

9 A stencil is also very useful for burnishing pigment in small areas, acting as a very precise yet movable mask. Here, the artist uses it to great effect as an aid to achieving the same burnished effect that he has in the sky, thereby creating a textural link throughout the whole composition.

10 *Texture predominates in this composition, created by directional burnishing and the exaggerated folds in the workers' clothing, providing a unity throughout the image. It invigorates the elements of the composition and at the same time heightens the sense of tension glimpsed in the faces of the men.*

Gallery

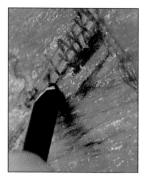

URBAN SCENE

The thickness of a pastel stick makes it more suited to a fairly coarse drawing style than to fine, detailed work. In this case the relative clumsiness of oil pastels has been turned to advantage. Broad, generalized color areas are contained by linear drawing to evoke the atmosphere of late evening. Dark tones created by a series of vigorously overlaid colors are occasionally relieved by small areas of bright color that represent the clarity of a lighted window shining through the twilight. The linear form of a giant crane rising on the skyline behind the buildings is treated with the finer marks made by a pastel pencil. The structure cuts across the grain of the underlying blue pastel marks.

PENCIL AND WASH STUDY OF TRAFALGAR SQUARE, LONDON

This piece is very much in the tradition of typographical art. It accurately records an aspect of Trafalgar Square without really making any comment about the life of the city. The same style of drawing could be used to depict any city.

STILL LIFE

Still life need not be the dull subject that it is often thought to be. Still life drawings can be created from everyday objects of life, often with strikingly attractive results. To capture the form and relationship of a group of pots, pans, jars, and fruits—the traditional components of still life—as and where they occur is frequently highly rewarding. An alternative is to mount a deliberately staged arrangement of objects.

Choosing your subject

Domestic subjects give you ready-made material for your sketches and the opportunity to work out the visual problems and possibilities at greater leisure. If you select subjects around your own home, you can work longer term on the same theme than you can with an outdoor subject, whether this involves making a series of sketches relating to the same object or view, or more in-depth color studies, for example. There is a very wide range of subject matter to be found in any furnished room. The general structure of the interior architecture is one: its overall planes introduce the basics of perspective drawing;

INK AND WATERCOLOR
by Stan Smith

Glass is a fascinating subject for still life study, the patterns made by its transmitted light creating unusual detail within a simple structure. There is a pleasing symmetry to the composition created by this straight row of bottles, within which the artist gives free rein to the colors and textures.

windows and doors may crate areas of texture, unusual light effects, and glimpses of views through and beyond the room into adjacent spaces that give depth and visual interest to a sketch composition.

The way furniture is grouped in the room provided various incidental still lifes; the hard textures and surface values of wood, plastic, and metal from which furniture is made contrast with the fluid forms and gentle contours of soft furnishings—curtains, cushions, and rugs. These often provide pleasing elements of pattern that can enliven your sketches with their varied shapes and colors.

EVERYDAY ARRANGEMENT
by Daphne Casdagli

This is just the kind of ordinary sight that might meet your eyes as you enter any room. The arrangement of table and chairs has been treated as a tonal study, contrasting cool grays with warm brown tones. This interpretation gives the drawing a somber mood of its own beyond the everyday character of the subject.

STILL LIFE
by Jan McKenzie

There is a delicate balance between line and mass in this still life by Jan McKenzie, and a good balance between the cold blue and warm orange hues. The symmetry of the central subject is offset by the arrangement of pattern detail in the background.

Plants, flower arrangements, ornaments, and fruit bowls may be immediately recognizable as appealing subjects for still life, but don't neglect the more familiar and mundane possessions in your home that can create exciting individual or group sketches. A jumble of randomly used kitchen implements lying on a worktop; food packets spilling from a supermarket bag; garden tools standing by the back door; the brushes, paints, and crayons lying about in your studio; discarded clothes lying on a bed or chair.

Because these are functional rather than decorative elements, it is easy to overlook their visual potential. And any subject is useful practice for sketching techniques: try out materials and methods that you do not normally use or that you cannot investigate fully in other situations—pastels, paints, and even collaged elements.

In your search for subject matter a viewing frame can be very useful. Do as many drawings as you can to practice looking for subject matter. Do not be too selective: do not think that what is familiar to you is not worth the effort to draw. One of the great problems that the beginner has in still life is indecision over what to draw. Such indecision is often caused by the fact that to make a drawing demands a considerable effort from beginners and they therefore feel that their view must be directed toward a subject that

PEACHES
by Martin Davidson

The peaches for this still life drawing were lit from above to emphasize the highlights on the soft, downy skin. The pastel was done on a rough, light gray paper, with layers of color built up and sprayed with fixative at regular intervals. The final strokes of pastel were only lightly fixed, thus retaining the freshness of color.

PASTEL EXERCISE

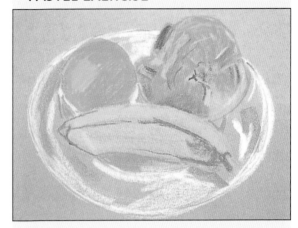

1 *The artist has chosen neutral gray to bring out the bright color of each objects. She begins by loosely blocking in the main forms of the fruit, pepper, and plate.*

2,3 *She can now tackle the individual textures. The slightly rough waxy surface and broken highlights of the orange are rendered with short, stabbing strokes, while for the banana and pepper she allows the pastel stick to smoothly follow the form.*

EXPERT TIP

Try drawing the kitchen worktop—just as it is. Don't bother to clear away the random clutter of utensils and food packets, their shapes, patterns, and textures form a fascinating still life.

warrants such effort on their part. This results in their simply dismissing highly pictorial subjects because the assumed status of the view in front of them does not appear to warrant the effort involved. The commonplace object can nevertheless become a special, highly interesting, and emotively charged objected when drawn by an artist.

Once again, it is the age-old problem of seeing the pictorial possibilities of what is around you all the time. Things change by the light in which they are seen. The play of light is one of the most important elements, and the shapes and colors of objects change constantly under the effect of changing light.

Marian Carrigan allows bright color and pattern variation to delineate form. The choice of subject illustrates the way strikingly original images can be found in everyday situations, if the artist is alert to the design potential of chance arrangements.

Composing your still life

SUNNY WINDOW
by Hugh Barnden

Hugh Barnden's sunny window view maintains a high-key range of color— yellow, blue, and mauve—and uses linear detail to define the structure of the composition. The geometric lines of the windows and the decorative balcony rail are traced on a warm mid-tone against the cool tints of the color blocks.

One of the best pieces of advice when drawing still life is to study the range of foods and objects on a table during or after a meal. Whether it was a boiled egg and a piece of toast or the remains of a three-course meal, the range of subjects seemed endless, while the rather haphazard arrangement of the food and other objects often suggested interesting and natural-looking compositions. In general, a still life should not look too "posed," but the casual look that can only be achieved by careful arrangements of objects. Most painters or drawers of still life will spend a considerable amount of time carefully considering the options before deciding to start a painting, experimenting by bringing in objects, removing others, and adjusting groupings— always looking to the main overall composition.

For the beginner it is always best to start off with a limited number of objects—perhaps no more than five or six—and to arrange them in a simple composition.

In choosing the objects for your drawing, pay

the color range, and finally redeveloping the pattern of light and shade. This approach is simply demonstrated with felt-tip pens.

EXERCISE IN COMPOSITION

This sequence shows stages in an exercise in composition, first establishing line and tone, next introducing local color, then extending

special attention to the contrast and balance of different textures, so that you can juxtapose smooth with rough, shiny with matt, and hard with soft.

The more visual excitement and contrast you can introduce into the subject the more challenging it will become and the more you will be able to get out of it. But don't overdo it; just as in a play or film, too many contrasts and dramatic juxtapositions will tend to confuse the viewer.

The drawing below is in pen and ink, which demands a more methodical approach than pencil. A loose crosshatching has been used to control the tones, with a variety of marks, including light scribbling, delineating the shiny skin and dark markings. The form is hinted at by a few small parallel lines near the lower line of the fish.

EXPERT TIP
Starting with a monochrome drawing can be an excellent way of gaining familiarity with textures. Because you are denied the luxury of color you are forced to observe very closely and use your ingenuity to find marks that will convey what you see. Pencil is a good medium to begin with, as it combines precision with great flexibility. Here the artist has started with a clear linear contour within which light hatching and scribbles suggest the elusive reflective surfaces.

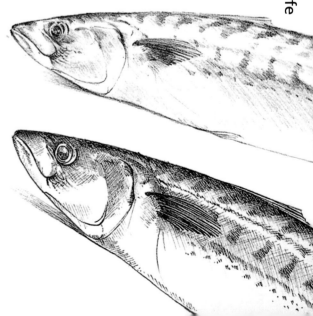

Interior light

As compared to outdoor light, the light sources within an interior are more readily controlled by the artist, although it is often a chance effect of daylight entering a room that provides the idea for an effective composition. However, there can be great variety in the color quality and intensity of the light, depending on whether it comes from a natural or artificial source.

Whereas you may have strong natural light at a window, the level falls quickly further into the room. In two studies here (opposite page), the artist describes brilliant light from a large window complemented by a smaller pool of lamplight focused on the shadowed work area. These provide interesting patterns of light and shade enhanced in one case by the central focus

of the window frame, in the other by the slatted blind drawn down over the window.

Smaller studies, on page 166, deal with the enclosing effect of concentrated lamplight, which draws in the space of the room and creates a warm glow. This effect has been interpreted in loose watercolor washes overlaid with crayon and pencil work, and in a colored pencil rendering with an atmospheric, grainy texture.

The linear pattern of the louvered blind is exploited in the third small sketch (bottom) and its effect is highlighting the objects standing in front of the window.

Bottle and glass

Everywhere your eye falls possible still life subjects come to light. Remember, though, that this vast potential brings obvious pitfalls in its wake. An obvious trap is that of making a fleetingly glimpsed, fortuitous arrangement substitute for a well thought out and balanced design, even though the former has its own charm and energy. When the eye takes in a picture, it is the organization—that is, the relationships of shape, size, and texture—that is the first to be seen and appreciated. This is the abstract element every picture possesses, one that is always present and that any artist disregards at his or her peril.

Always consider carefully the relative scale of what you are drawing. Whatever you choose, each element will have at least two roles to play—as an object containing its own characteristics of weight, shape, form and so on and as part of the whole. Another trick to bear in mind is to offset an area of intense visual activity with calm, simple patches of tone. This, too, will heighten your composition's interest by introducing a feeling of contrast.

1 *Take care when making your initial drawing—it is difficult to make each side of the bottle and glass the same as the other.*

2 *Start to build up color, using your finger to smudge and blend a number of colors together and work areas of lights and darks.*

3 *A light background defines the dark shapes of the glass and bottle, emphasizing the tension between them—they are similar, but the glass is smaller and rounder.*

4 *Work shadows and reflections on the glass and bottle; there is nothing mysterious about reflections—just keep looking hard to see where highlights should go.*

Left, putting in the ground color, avoiding the area of the base of the bottle and glass and rubbing it into the paper with your finger.

Right, using a dark color to put in shadow on the stem of the glass.

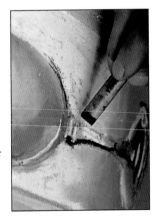

Still life with tulips

1 *Concentrating on the color theme of the still life the artist begins by blocking in the largest area of red, using it as a ground and as a key for working up the rest of the picture.*

For this still life the artist chose just a few objects—an apple, a lemon, a wrapped bunch of tulips and irises, and a sketchbook. Each element in this small arrangement has a different texture, color, and form from the next, to add interest to the group: the apple is a smooth, deep red, streaked and flecked with light red and orange; the pitted surface of the lemon and its vivid color provide a high contrast to the apple; the simple, heavy forms of the fruit are offset by the fussy lettering on the wrapping paper; the green letters and the striated leaves complement the apple's red just as the blue of the irises and the shadows complement the yellow lemon. The sketchbook on which the fruit is placed is used to anchor them in the image—without it they would appear to be floating in mid-air.

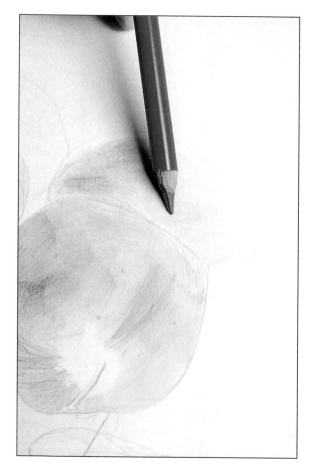

2 *Working around the apple, she establishes its form in its environment by ghosting in a blue shadow behind it.*

3 *The yellow of the lemon is developed further, strengthening the triangle of primary colors. This group of forms and colors creates a point of reference from which later decisions about color can be made.*

4 *Using a soft eraser, the base colors are worked and blended into the paper's surface to create a very fine, smooth texture. This texture will later contrast with strong strokes worked over the blended colors.*

5 *Using bold strokes of purple and dark red applied with considerable pressure, the streaky texture of the apple skin is indicated. These strokes stand out particularly strongly against the smooth background.*

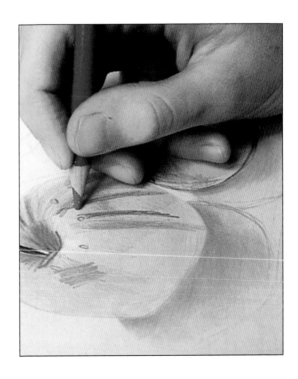

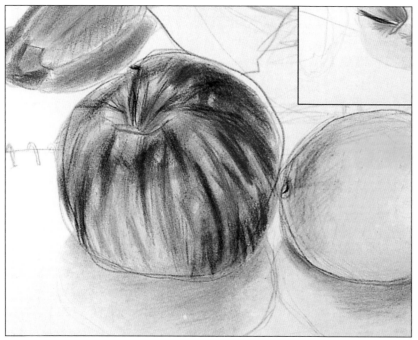

6 *The different reds and the strokes used on the apple give it form. A hint of red is also applied to the lemon to indicate its slightly reflective surface. Slowly the red elements of the composition come together, linking the whole image.*

7 *Fine blue lines are drawn over the green base color of the leaves, the direction of the strokes creating a sense of movement in sympathy with their structure and form.*

8 *Pale cream laid over and between darker hues conveys the glazed effect of the cellophane wrapping paper.*

9 *The soft, floating colors of this work are anchored by lines that weave in and out of them, delineating shape while suggesting movement and life. There is nothing still about this still life!*

Project 12: Still life with tulips

Still life with shells

The patterns on this bag decorated with shells have an abstract quality that the artist decided to explore in her drawing. Using faint pink lines she mapped out general guidelines for shape and color. Taking two of the predominant hues in the still life she then laid the first patch of color and built up the other colors around and in direct relationship to it systematically. Gradually the whole image area was blocked in. Using sketch-like lines and areas of tone that bleed over their boundaries, or fall short of these limits, the lighter colors were laid in such a way that they seem to be floating. Shadows have been picked out in blues, running across the darker areas, linking and blending colors. The three-dimensional aspects of this still life have been treated as lines—lines of color, lines of texture, and lines of shape—that move and suggest potential dimension but that are themselves flat.

1 *The rich shapes, textures, colors, and patterns in this small embroidered purse adorned with shells inspired the artist to investigate the visual complexities of this still life.*

2 *Using pale pink, faint guidelines were sketched in, and then the colors of each item were added.*

3 *Having laid the ground color, the drawing is reworked with rich, heavy colors, deep into the paper's surface.*

4 *Working from the point at which the handkerchief and the purse meet—an ideal key for color reference—the artist now moves farther out, slowly and gradually.*

5 *The elements of the composition, particularly the shadows, are treated as decorative devices. Here, a Prussian blue is used to suggest shadow, a colorful and exciting interpretation of reality.*

6 *The final work is a riot of colored areas floating approximately within the guide of the fluid outlines. Many of the colors are laid over others; for example, in some places the artist has laid red-brown over yellow, allowing the yellow to glimmer through. Every object has a linear and tonal shape. The juxtaposition of solid areas of strokes and simple lines creates a wonderfully fresh feeling of freedom of color.*

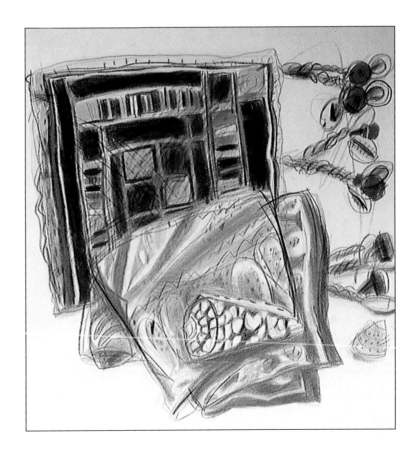

Irises

An almost monochromatic scene has been injected with life by a shaft of life piercing through the window. The vivid purple and yellow of the iris flowers positively glow in this cool room where time seems to stand still. Beyond is the hint of a warmer world—inside, large cold spaces that take their life from the texture of the hatching only stand poised, like the black table wedge that is cantilevered across the middle foreground, anchored by the edge of the paper. The whole composition has a strong linear quality, which embodies a tension that is released only in the flowers.

1 *In this photograph a shaft of light through a window illuminates a cool shadowy interior, always an exciting temptation to the artist. Such natural spotlights create beautiful extremes in lights and darks.*

2 *Having sketched in the basic framework of the picture in deep gray, the artist then concentrated on the focal point—the flowerheads—working up the intricate color planes en masse. He used ultramarine, dark violet, light violet, and Prussian blue.*

3 *Color was applied to the flowers using broad, strong strokes, starting with the palest color and working through to the darker hues. Spaces were left for the finishing highlights of Naples yellow.*

4 *The shadowy monochromatic background is too plain to be treated as a totally flat expanse of one color, so a complex stroke pattern of hatching and cross-hatching is applied to create texture within the color, quite independently of the paper's surface.*

5 *The large areas of hatched background above and to the left of the vase of flowers are treated as balancing areas of tone within the composition, pivoting on the diagonal.*

6 *The visual balance is substantiated by balancing the vase of flowers on the "fulcrum" on the table. Beneath the table surface a dark area of cross-hatched black is added as a balance to the dark hues in the greenery of the flowers. The hard edge of the table was created by hatching against a ruler.*

7 *The intricate geometric patterns created by the stems of the flowers and their reflections in the glass vase are treated as a collection of colored shapes. Unlike the background, which is handled very gently, heavy pressure is used here to give force to the main elements of the composition and make them stand out from the background.*

8 *Silver gray, blue gray, raw sienna, and raw umber are hatched over the glass areas of the window, the strokes made in one direction and applied very evenly, with consistent, though light, pressure.*

9 *The areas of glass are worked over with a putty eraser using long strokes to remove some pigment and smooth out what remains. This leaves slanted areas of white paper showing through the color, which indicate the reflective nature of the glass surface.*

10 *The finished drawing shows how the hatched background is cleverly given its own texture and interest and contains much more dimension that it would as a flat color. At the same time it offers a superb foil to the heavier, tightly worked elements of the composition.*

Magic!

The artist in this case is an amateur magician, which is why she chose these subjects for her still life. She has carefully constructed this work on a skeleton of lines. Applying colors in a sequence, the image was built up to describe, in terms of color, a world of shape. We even look at the top h at as a negative shape—from the inside out—and similarly the hat and gloves form a white silhouette against a sea of color. The whole picture is a study in positively applied color creating negative forms. Even the angle at which the still life is viewed extends this approach by throwing forward a very three-dimensional object from a considerably flatter background. The depth is as illusory as the trickery it depicts!

THE FINISHED IMAGE

It is only when all the elements are in place that the shape of the colors add form to the completed still life drawing. Although shadows have been drawing in over the existing colors, the structure of the picture is still fairly flat. It relies heavily on the artist's ability to abstract color and form to create dimensions.

1 *Using a color that will be present in all the major elements of the drawing the artist has sketched in an underdrawing with positive lines as a skeleton on which to build color.*

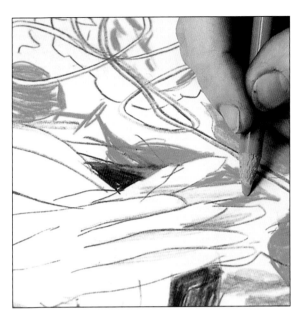

2 *The artist now lays in an area of green. Some black has also been used in particularly dark areas, to create a balance next to the white focal center of the composition—the magician's glove.*

3 *Two small points of red are drawn in—the tip of the wand and the fold of the scarf—to be developed later.*

4 *The red heightens its complementary, green, as it is worked around the colored shapes. The bold, heavy strokes give the color a density which exaggerates the pattern and decorative qualities of the image.*

Still life with onions

The striations on the translucent layers of onion skin are an ideal pattern to depict using impressed line. The artist traced the outline of the onions and their markings on tracing paper laid over the final drawing surface, pressing hard with a graphite pencil. The depressions left in the paper became an integral part of the finished drawings. It is important to envisage the final structure of the color composition before you start impressing because impressed lines are not easy to remove or disguise.

1 *After outlining the form of the onions on the drawing surface in brown pencil, the artist then laid tracing paper and, with a graphite pencil, drew the lines of the onions, pressing hard on the paper.*

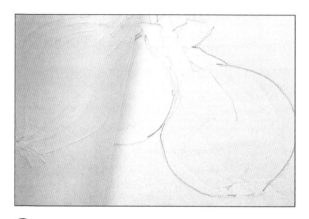

2 *When the lines are all drawn the artist removes the tracing paper and reveals a network of indented gulleys in the surface of the paper. These impressed lines become an inherent part of the image and will alter the visual effects of any colored pigment applied later.*

3 *Greens and browns are added to the forms, applied parallel to and across the impressed lines to exaggerate their appearance.*

EXPERT TIP
Create a still life of objects with well-defined outlines—for instance, a collection of china dishes, cups and jugs, or a group of fruits or vegetables. Sketch them by defining on your paper the shapes between and around them, rather than the shapes of the objects themselves.

4 *As more pigment is added, the lines become more dominant—only where color is very heavily pressured does it penetrate the impressions.*

5 *Hatched areas of impressed line emphasize the papery quality of the dried onion skin and its surface pattern.*

6 *The finished drawing shows how successfully color and form can be emphasized with impressed lines. The lines on the halved onion parallel the contours on the skin of the whole onion, creating a natural harmony.*

Upside down objects

A way of banishing our preconceived ideas about an object is to place it in an unfamiliar situation. In art schools elaborate groups are sometimes constructed to present familiar objects in unusual ways. This is a very valuable draawing experience, and worth trying for yourself, but you can achieve the same result by simply turning an object upside down.

Choose an object such as a stool, a chair, or an ironing board, or something much smaller like a plate rack, and turn it upside down on the floor or on a table. The object needs to be something that is fairly complicated but with a construction that is easy to identify. Make a drawing in line, color, or line and tone as you wish. This time draw the object itself but don't forget the importance of the negative shapes, as they are a very useful drawing aid. As you draw, from time to time turn your drwing upside down (right way up) and see how it looks, but resist the temptation to continue drawing it the correct way up. When you have finished, place the drawing upside down (right way up) for viewing.

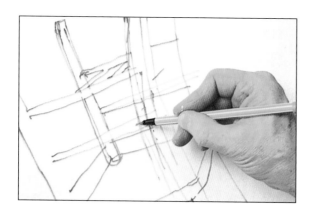

1 *The drawing has been started in line, drawn with a colored water-soluble marker. This particular color was chosen because it will later be used to describe the color of the chair. Attention has been paid both to the negative shapes and the abstract pattern of the chair.*

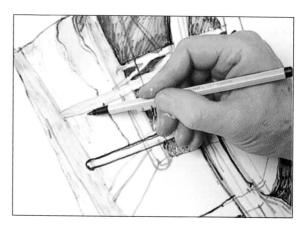

2 *A darker marker is now used to shade in the background and re-state and strengthen some of the lines describing the chair.*

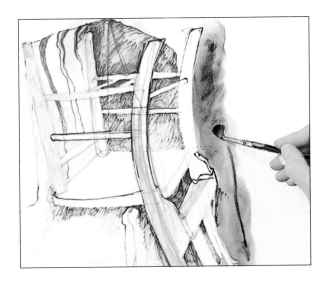

3 *The crimson stripes have been reinforced and a wetted brush used to spread the marker ink into a wash for the background area.*

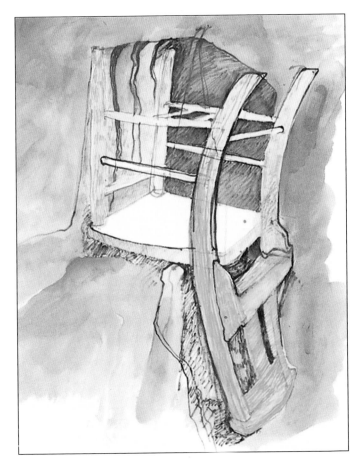

4 *It is easier to concentrate on the abstract qualities of an object when it is seen in an unfamiliar context or upside down, as in this case.*

EXPERT TIP
First try drawing the object the right way up and then upside down. Be self-critical and ask yourself the following questions:

- *Does the object look convincing?*

- *Did you find it easier to draw the object upside down, or did you find that you had to constantly turn your board?*

- *Did you find it easier to produce an accurate drawing this way?*

Almost certainly your second attempt will be more accurate, because once the drawing is upside down you forget what the objects in it are, and concentrate on the abstract shapes.

Shading and burnishing

Colored pencils, being easy to handle as well asa light and portable, are an excellent medium for drawing still life. They can also achieve intricate, highly detailed effects and rich blends of color. In most colored pencil drawings, tones and colors are built up by various methods of overlaying, such as hatching, cross-hatching, and shading. Shading can also be used for mixing and modifying colors. One layer of shading can be laid over another to achieve a softer effect than is attained by hatching.

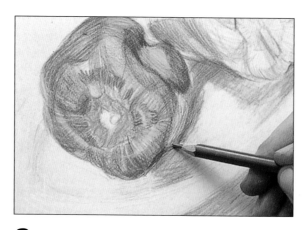

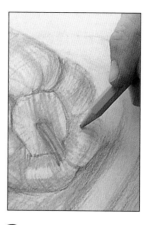

1 *The artist begins by laying in the colors lightly, leaving certain areas of the paper white for the highlights.*

2 *The dark shadow is now added. With this in place, the artist will be better able to judge how much further shading is needed to build up the colors of the vegetables.*

3 *As in hatching and cross-hatching, shading lines can take any direction you choose. Here the pencils follow the forms of the vegetables.*

4 *In the final stages, the reds and greens were built up more densely by further shading. In the highlight areas the paper has been left uncovered or only very lightly covered, while in the areas of deepest color the paper is no longer visible.*

Burnishing is a technique sometimes used to increase the brilliance of colors. After the colors has been mixed on the paper, the surface is rubbed with a finger or a rag to produce a slight sheen.

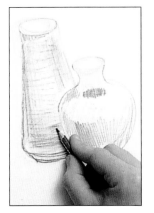 

1 *Burnishing is always a final stage in a drawing; first all the colors must be established and built up as thickly as desired (left). The artist continues to lay colors, using a combination of the shading and hatching techniques. Notice that on the body of the green vase he has used curving lines that follow the contours (right).*

4 *The bottom lip of the small vase is now darkened; it is in shadow because it curves away and under the body of the pot. The shiny, reflective surfaces of the objects have allowed the artist to introduce a wide range of colors.*

2 *A very dark blue pencil is now used to press the color into the paper, creating a small area of dark reflection. On reflective surfaces, tonal changes are often very abrupt, with a distinct, hard-edged boundary between one tone and color and another.*

3 *In this area of the pot's surface, the colors merge more gently, so the artist "pushes" the colors into one another and into the paper by rubbing with a torchon.*

5 *The contrast between the rich burnished colors and the sparkling highlights creates a convincing impression of the pot's shiny surface.*

Building up and blending

If you are using a fairly small range of colors and want to achieve subtle effects or rich, dark hues, you will have to "mix" colors on the paper by overlaying. The hatching and cross-hatching methods used in colored pencil drawing are also suitable for the whole range of pastels. For broad effects made with side strokes you can overlay colors more directly, simply by putting one stroke over another. If you are working on heavily textured paper, you can make a good many such overlays, but lighte rpaper will become clogged with pigment more quickly, and you may need to spray with fixative between layers.

1 *This artist works mainly in colored pencil, and he uses pastel in a similar way, laying a series of firm hatched lines.*

2 *He now introduces darker colors, using the same method.*

3 *Notice how the direction of the lines has been varied to express the forms of the bottle and the two separate horizontal planes.*

BLENDING

The color-mixing technique particularly associated with pastel work is blending, in which two or more colors are laid over one another and then rubbed with a cotton ball, your fingers, or a torchon (good for small areas) so that they fuse together. This method allows you to achieve almost any color or tone, but it is not wise to overdo blending, as it can make your drawing look bland and insipid. You will often need to blend colors in some areas of a drawing, but try to combine the technique with vigorous lines, or fix the blended color and draw over it.

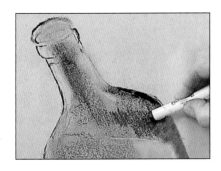

1 *The artist works in a completely different way, rubbing the colors into the paper to create a soft effect. Here she modifies the green with a touch of white.*

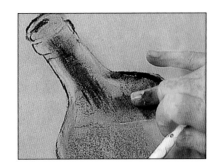

2 *Rubbing with a finger blends one color into another. A gray paper (the "wrong" side of Mi-Teintes) has been chosen, as this makes it easier to judge both the darks and lights.*

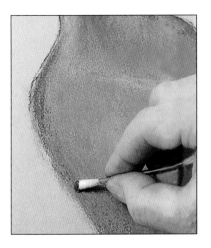

3 *A finger would be too clumsy an emplement for the blending on the side of the bottle, so a cotton bud is used. The artist prefers these to torchons, as they are softer and have a gentler action.*

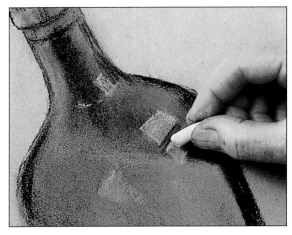

4 *Because pastels are opaque, light colors can be laid over dark ones provided there is not too much build-up of color on the paper surface. The highlights are thus left until last.*

5 *This makes an interesting contrast with the demonstration opposite; here there are no visible lines. The two methods can be combined in one drawing.*

Gallery

CHRISTMAS TINS
by Jenny Tilden-Wright

Colored pencil drawings are no longer the domain solely of children, nor are they regarded merely as preparatory stages in the execution of a work of art. Today they are a popular medium for illustration, particularly in the area of packaging.

FRESH CREAM CAKES
by Simon Thompson

_In this drawing of fresh cream cakes, the artist has used hatching and cross-hatching throughout
his work to create unique texture and color. The flaky, crisp texture of the pastry and the papery
quality of the cases are made even more contincing by his deft use of hatching._

VEGETABLES
by Madeleine David

Nicely regimented lines of vegetables have a vigorous character due to the freely worked texture of the colored pencil drawing in which the artist has used an inventive approach to building the color mixtures. The yellows and browns in the onions are worked over soft purple shading, with strong white highlights overlaid to simulate the shiny skins. Dark-toned blues give extra brightness to the natural yellow-greens of the leeks.

PLANTS AND FLOWERS

From Egyptian tomb paintings and jewelry to Greek pottery, the value placed on flowers in early decorative art is apparent. Varied textures, colors, and shapes all make plants and flowers one of the most attractive and challenging artistic subjects.

Choosing your subject

Plant and flower drawing is both enjoyable and extremely challenging; somehow it must suggest the continuing life of the subject while ensuring great fidelity in the detailing of leaf, petal, and flower. A major consideration should be the retention of the overall solid form, while describing the fragile, intricate quality of petal and leaf. The fold of form over form in petals and of interlocking and interchanging planes in leaves must all be expressed and explained. Close observation is the clue to achieving the best results.

The spectrum of what you can draw ranges widely; you can choose to create a simple study of a single flower, or, at a more ambitious level, you might decide to draw a complex, sprawling ivy, or a complicated flower arrangement. Whichever you choose, remember that plant drawing is a mixture of still life and natural history. Obviously, you can set up many subjects in the studio, but, at the same time, you should

CHRYSANTHEMUMS
by Kay Gallwey

This is a wonderfully spirited pastel, full of movement and life. The yellow flowers are beautifully summarized with the minimum of colors.

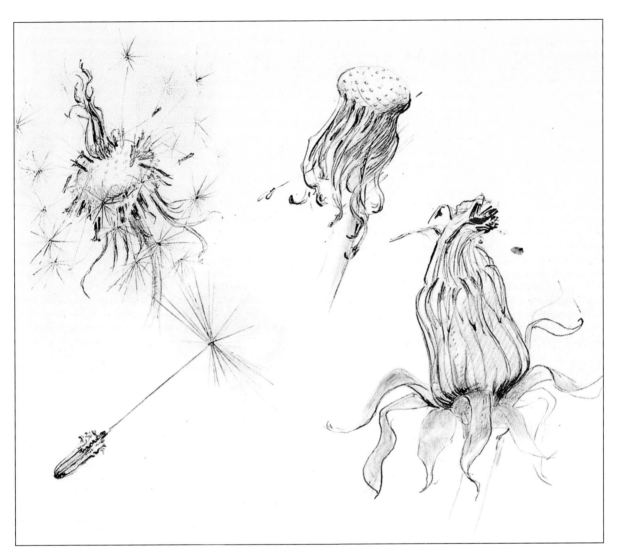

never forget that what you are drawing is a living thing and should be rendered as such. One of the best things to try is putting the plant—your main subject—into the most natural setting you can find. The surrounding colors will frequently make the final study more sympathetic.

Pencil is the ideal base medium, since its use will enable you to achieve high standards of draftsmanship. The tool gives you the ability to capture the intricacies of detail and so analyze the problems of shape and form. Make the best possible use of the chosen support, allowing the plant almost to "grow" upward and outward across its surface. Use color sparingly, but decisively, making the fullet possible use of the resources of mixed media. A slight descriptive touch of local color, for instance, can enliven the study of something as simple as a rose twig.

STUDY IN PENCIL AND CRAYON
by Elisabeth Harden

An unusual technique was involved in creating the downy plant spores in the lefthand image (above). The pattern of fine filaments was etched into the paper surface using the edge of a key, then graphite from a 6B pencil was lightly rubbed over the area, leaving the impressed lines showing white through the surrounding light gray tone.

Broom

This is a very simple line and wash drawing by Margaret Stevens, with later additions of colored and water-soluble pencils.

1 *A pot of broom suggests summer on a February day.*

2 *A single flowering spray is very quickly drawn using a 0.3mm technical pen.*

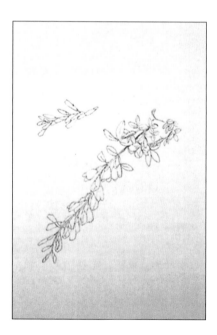

3 *As it is not intended to portray the entire plant, a second spray most suited to its position is added.*

4 *The desired shape of the composition is gradually achieved.*

5 *The artist adds a pale wash of blue watercolor behind the blooms.*

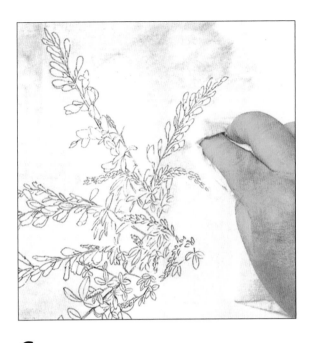

6 *Soft paper towel is used to dab out a cloud effect.*

7 *A wash of pale aureolin yellow is applied to the flowers with a little Indian yellow to provide simple shading.*

9 *You can now see the overall effect.*

8 *The tiny leaves are washed over with a pale bluish-green.*

10 *The artist uses a watercolor pencil in night green to give depth at the base of the plant.*

11 *This deep color is blended in with water using a fine sable brush.*

12 *Later the picture is finished by the addition of a rocky outcrop executed in watercolor and colored pencils. Further sprays of broom extend the plant and additional cross-hatching in ink intensifies the shadows.*

PROJECT 21 Seedheads

This drawing by Hilary Leigh illustrates what can be achieved by using colored inks with a simple mapping pen, to portray very simple plant material.

1 *These seedheads were collected in summer and left to dry naturally.*

2 *Two stems of dock are drawn, using burnt sienna ink, to establish the upper limits of the picture.*

3 *The artist uses purple to draw a head of cow parsley, partly in front of the dock.*

4 *Purple is used again to add detail to a yellow umbelliferous seedhead.*

5 *The basic structure of the picture is now established.*

6 *The artist begins to fill in the main body of the picture with further stems, but keeping to the brown, yellow, and purple shades.*

8 *You can see how the body of the composition has started to fill out.*

7 *A brush is used to run in a well-diluted mix of yellow and Prussian blue, which makes an attractive green, and gives an impression of hazy depth.*

9 *The artist has called on her memory of summer by including the moon daisies, and now the center of the drawing is being worked on to give a more intense tone.*

10 *Stems are being finished off and an additional daisy gives interest at the bottom of the picture.*

11 *A final touch of detail is added to a woody stem.*

12 *The finished drawing is an harmonious blend of very few colors, inspired by a basic collection of what would commonly be called weeds.*

Marigolds

This drawing by Hilary Leigh in soft pastels on Ingres paper, aims to catch the Provençal brilliance of the flowers. The vase of marigolds (*below left*) is the basic subject and will be rearranged on paper to produce an interesting composition.

1 *The first flowers are positioned using pale cadmium yellow soft pastel.*

2 *The artist freely sketches in leaves, stems, and some detail of the flowers.*

3 *Various shades of yellow and orange are used to portray the color of the petals.*

4 *The first green is added, with lizard green giving the foundation color.*

5 *Prussian blue has been used to give the deepest tone between the flowers.*

6 *The overall composition has now taken shape.*

7 *The artist uses her fingers to blend Prussian blue and mid-tone purple at the top of the drawing.*

8 *More work is done on the foliage, using a mix of lizard, sap, and olive green.*

9 *The background is extended, with the purple-blue tone throwing the golden flowers forward.*

10 *The artist turns her attention to the central cluster of blooms.*

11 *More background is added and again fingers merge the colors.*

EXPERT TIP

Try investigating the structures and patterns in natural subjects that are indicative of their growth and function. These basic frameworks provide information on systems of design in nature that can provide inspiration for development of other images and even the design of objects.

12 *Detail at the center of the marigold is achieved by using madder brown.*

13 *The finished picture exudes all the warmth and vitality of the Mediterranean.*

Anemones

This drawing by Hilary Leigh is made with watersoluble pencils on a good quality watercolor paper. Two bunches of anemones provide the inspiration for this study that is not intended to be exact reproduction.

1 *The artist draws an initial outline using a deep vermilion pencil.*

2 *The color is merged with water applied with a fine brush.*

3 *Detail at the center of the flower is achieved by using a mixture of dark violet, burnt umber, and burnt carmine.*

4 *Intensity of color is built up by applying more dry pencil on top of the pre-washed sections. This dry, wet, dry, wet technique applies throughout.*

5 *The pattern of color is established by introducing mauve flowers between the reds.*

6 *Fine-cut foliage is worked on, using an initial May green followed by sap, olive, juniper, and cedar.*

7 *Detail is brought out on the central mauve flower using blue violet, light violet, and Imperial purple.*

8 *The artist adds a bud at the top of the drawing, extending the stem to improve the composition.*

9 *Depth is achieved by using an indigo pencil, dipped in water, which gives the darkest tone to the center of the study.*

10 *The half-moon composition is filled out by adding a semi-profiled flower at top right.*

11 *The composition is extended further with an opening bud at the bottom right to lead the eye downward.*

12 *Darker tones are added to give stability at the base of the picture.*

13 *Final touches of color have been added to capture the glowing colors of the flowers.*

Irises and hyacinth

The rich blues of these flowers are ideal for a drawing using colored pencils on a support of NOT watercolor paper.

1 *Time does not allow all these beautiful flowers to be portrayed.*

2 *The artist first makes an outline drawing of the iris using light ultramarine. Zinc yellow shading is added and deep cobalt is used to shade the petals.*

3 *A mix of deep cobalt and Prussian blue is used to contour the petals, with purple adding the deepest tone.*

4 *A little carmine supplies the pinkish tinge where it is needed.*

5 *Ocher over zinc yellow shades the falls. You will see that no attempt has yet been made to position stems or leaves.*

6 *The hyacinth is drawn in to cut across the front of the irises. The stem uses an interesting mix of Hooker's green, red violet, and deep cobalt.*

7 *The flowers are worked up using similar tones to the iris, but with less deep blue and more carmine and purple.*

8 *The stems have been added using a mixture of zinc yellow, moss green, and Hooker's green. Now dark touches of detail are added to the hyacinth bells.*

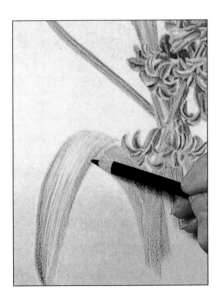

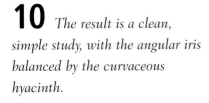

9 *The imposing curve of the hyacinth leaf is contoured with slight touches of dark gray.*

10 *The result is a clean, simple study, with the angular iris balanced by the curvaceous hyacinth.*

Iris

1 *A perfect iris is the ideal specimen for an exercise in ink. Margaret Stevens demonstrates the stippling technique used in botanical drawings.*

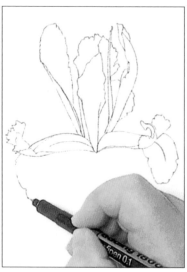

2 *The artist makes an initial drawing using a 0.3mm technical pen. Every effort is made to achieve accuracy in positioning the petals.*

3 *The first lines of dots, which model the curves of the flower, are drawn.*

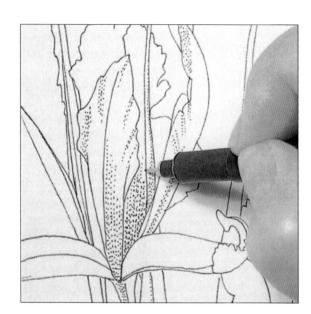

4 *Further dots are added to mold the curve to the right shape.*

5 *The artist stipples the fall of a petal, showings its crinkly edge.*

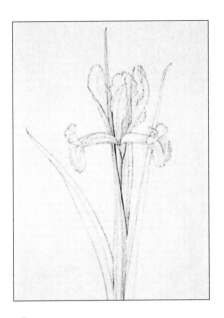

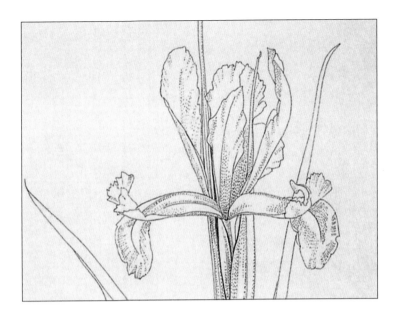

6 *You can now see the overall appearance of the iris at around the halfway point.*

7 *This close-up of the actual flower shows you the amount of stippling necessary to indicate the form of the bloom—not its color!*

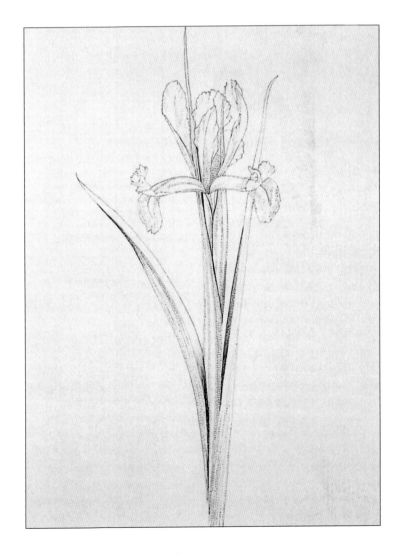

8 *The artist works long rows of dots following the straight line of the leaf. These are overlaid as necessary with other rows of dots, to build up a degree of depth.*

9 *The finished flower study should be clean, simple, and accurate.*

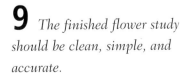

DRAWING PEOPLE

There can be few more satisfactory achievements than making a drawing of a figure, attempting to express its individuality, character, and style. Never be discouraged if your early attempts seem far from successful; practice is the only route to better results and a classic method of learning is to continue to work at and improve your less than satisfactory drawings, rather than simply throwing them away and starting again.

The basics

Drawing people obeys the same basic rules of drawing as for any other subject matter: the problem still consists of translating what is three-dimensional onto a two-dimensional surface. But to most beginners, and even to artists of some experience, the problem of drawing the figure appears to be insurmountable.

It is often incorrectly thought that the artist requires years of detailed anatomical study and of practice in drawing the figure from life before any satisfactory result can be achieved. This tends to make beginners avoid inclusion of any figure in their drawings and paintings wherever possible. Children, however, are in no way inhibited when it comes to making a representation of their parents, brothers, sisters, or teachers, and they quite freely make images of people that, although not photographic images, can be stunningly obvious.

PENCIL DRAWING
by Stan Smith

Especially when you are using a linear medium, tonal values do not have to be expressed as a solid mass or dense gradation. In this drawing the shading is applied very freely. It retains a linear quality while also conveying an impression of the continuous planes and volumes that shape the head and body.

HELEN
by Elaine Mills

Character and expression are important in any portrait drawing. The artist has relied on a quick color sketch to capture the spontaneity of the subject's smile and casual pose. The bright, warm pastel colors were used in a quick, vigorous manner to develop the texture and main features of the portrait.

To introduce yourself to drawing the figure, do not at first try to make an accurate representation as you might do in still life. Accuracy of observation is certainly still required, but for drawing the figure the student must begin to develop a visual memory. Unlike still life, the human figure is animated and moving for most of the time, so some system of retaining and then recording the particularities of people is required. The character of the person is seen not only on the face but also in the way in which he or she stands, walks, and moves the arms and head. Someone who is reasonably well known to you can be recognized from behind by the way in which he or she walks.

First practice drawing matchstick figures—but instead of drawing them in a childlike fashion, start considering where the joints of the arms and legs actually are. In this way, by observing people in their everyday activities and translating them into matchstick figures from memory, you will learn two of the most important elements in successful figure drawing. You will extend your visual memory, you will learn two of the most important elements in successful figure drawing. You will extend your visual memory and you will develop an understanding of animation.

Ask a friend or a member of your family to sit for you in as natural a pose as possible. Do not expect them to sit still for more than about ten minutes at a time, for it can become very uncomfortable and you could lose a potential model.

Work quickly, do a continuous line drawing in the same way as you would draw a tree. Do not try to draw the figure in its individual parts but draw the figure as a whole outline shape.

Our perceptual problems with the figure are far greater than they are with any other subject because we constantly refer to and think of people and ourselves in terms of the individual parts that make up the whole. We tend to think of somebody in terms of having a lovely face, nice hands, or big feet, as though these elements are totally unconnected with the person as a whole, because we appraise them as individual parts. This makes it difficult to get the individual parts in the correct proportion to one another when drawing the figure. For example, we naturally place far more importance on the head and face than we would on the feet or arms, because we communicate predominantly with the head and face. Every beginner therefore tends to draw the head proportionately much larger than it actually is. This can be seen in a drawing of a child, in which the body of the figure plays a very secondary role.

These sketches by Judy Martin investigate variations of mood in line by using felt-tip pens and markers, and in shaded color that has been applied with colored pencil.

Most of our experience of the figure takes place in a fully clothed situation, and it is sometimes difficult for the beginner to fully appreciate that inside a jacket sleeve is an arm, and about half way down the arm an elbow joint, and so on.

The next time you are in a public place, look at the people around you and make some rapid sketches in matchstick form of how the figures are articulated, making particular notes of knees, ankles, elbows, etc. For these matchstick figures really do work. Remember—the points of articulation must be in the right relationship and proportion to one another.

One area of figure drawing that has a particular appeal to a beginner is portraiture. As an art form, however, the photographer's work has to a large extent taken over the position formerly held by that of the representational portrait painter. When you first start drawing portraits, it is most important to draw your model in a direct and

honest manner, searching for the character of the sitter. The peculiarities of an individual's face—the difference between the left eye and the right eye, perhaps, and the realization that they are not identical—are more important to observe than the mere likeness. Even careful observation may not at first produce a truly representational drawing. Do not be over-concerned by this. It is yet again caused by the fact that it is all too easy to place too much importance on the individual elements that make up a face—the mouth, the eyes, the nose, etc.—and it is only a matter of getting these individual parts into their right relationship, and seeing the face and head as a whole.

PORTRAIT STUDY
by David Hockney

Drawings by David Hockney have had an important influence in stimulating a new appreciation of colored pencil as a major drawing medium. His portraits and figure studies have demonstrated how these simple tools acquire great sophistication and versatility in the hands of a master draftsman.

Hands

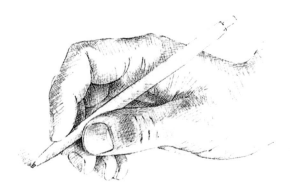

Drawing your own hand is excellent practice, and helps you to understand both the textures of skin and the underlying forms. If you find it difficult drawing your non-working hand, use a mirror and draw the reflection. In these pencil drawings the main form of the hand is contained by a precise linear contour, which has been completed by light shading. When adding tone to your drawing use the pencil experimentally to try out different effects.

Learning to draw hands is easier than it seems, as though they are complex forms, they become less daunting by simplifying the shapes. Hands can be a very important part of a drawing. The hard, marked, strong-fingered hand of a farm worker can imply a great deal about the character and life of the poser, as can the soft-formed hand of a young girl. Hands do present a number of problems in drawing; most of these are again, however, due to the way in which the hand is perceived. Although each finger has a certain expressiveness and fingers are commonly thought of individually—e.g. index finger, thumb —it is impossible to draw the hand one finger at a time, and it is only when the hand is seen as an overall shape, including the first three or four inches of the lower arm, that it can be success-fully tackled. A tree, after all, is easily perceived as an overall shape that is made up of a number of branches because it is thought of as one object. With the hand, the reverse is true. We think of it not as one shape or object, but as a combination of individual shapes or objects.

The hand, like the head, is a much larger object than most beginners think. Place the

bottom of the palm of your hand on your chin. You do not have to spread your fingers very widely to cover the majority of your face. But look at any untutored drawing and you will find that the hand is drawn as five very small fingers coming out of the end of the arm. The hand really begins some distance back from the wrist joint.

It is well worth a beginner's time to study the hand. This can be done by using your own hand: with the aid of a mirror the hand can be drawn

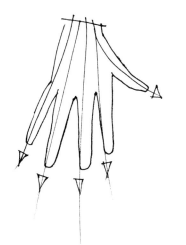

Note that the fingers radiate from the wrist (right), with the thumb in opposition. It is essential to observe and understand the range of movement of the thumb.

(Far right) When making initial sketches it is a good idea not to attempt to treat the fingers separately, but rather to draw their overall shape.

from various angles. Start by making a line drawing of the whole hand and then drawing into this shape the individual fingers and spaces in between them. What generally happens when drawing the hand is that you see only two or three of the fingers at one time. Carry on

drawing the hand in a variety of positions, concentrating on the whole shape. With a very limited knowledge of anatomy of the hand, plus intelligent observation, it will not take long before you feel confident including the hand as part of your portrait drawing.

MISS BOTINELLY
by Doug Dawson

This artist generally uses a restricted palette of three pastels—a dark, middle, and light tone—and then gradually builds up the colors to achieve an effect that has the expressive richness of an oil painting. Take special note of the position and size of the hands in this portrait.

Hair

There is such a range of textures and styles seen on the human head that it is impossible to generalize about them, but there are some points to bear in mind when you are drawing hair. The most important is to ensure that you relate the hair to the head itself. This sounds obvious, but if your subject has an elaborate hairstyle it is only too easy to become so involved in the intricacies of the curls and waves that you forget about the shape of the skull beneath and the way the hair relates to the face. Start by blocking in the main masses and then pay careful attention to the rhythms of the hair.

Look for the weight of the hair as this is important in giving shape to the style, even in the case of short hair. All hairstylists know that thick, heavy hair holds its shape better than thin, wispy hair, and the more shape it has the easier it is to draw. Thin, frizzy, or flyaway hair is trickier because it does not always follow the shape of the head very precisely, and is in general more demanding in terms of technique.

The final quality to look out for is the sheen of the hair. Dark, oily hair will have very pronounced highlights; thick, dry hair diffused ones, and thin, dry, or frizzy hair almost no recognizable highlight.

Pencil is a very sympathetic medium for drawing hair because of its ability both to capture the softest nuance of tone and to describe fine lines and rhythms. For long hair try sharpening the pencil to a fine, tapering point so that there is plenty of exposed lead and draw using the side and the point of the lead. Use a soft 2B pencil to begin with, and hold the pencil in a way that will give you sweeping moves with-

EXPERT TIP

To practice drawing hair, begin with a style that has clear shapes and forms—you can work from a photograph if you prefer. Ignore individual strands of hair and instead look for the main rhythms and movements, which you can simplify if necessary. Also look for the highlights and notice how they tend to move across the main flow of hair. Different drawing materials can also be useful in showing different textured hair. Pencil is good for soft effects, while conté crayon (below) gives greater depth and contrast.

DRAWING HAIR WITH PASTEL

1 *An off-white colored sheet of rough paper was chosen for this drawing, to act as a sympathetic background and also a basic skin tone.*

2 *The main shape and color of the hair is laid with the side of the pastel stick, while detail and movement are suggested with an ocher pastel used in a linear manner.*

3 *Here you can see how the texture of the paper plays an important role in the drawing, breaking up the pastel strokes.*

(Left) The movement of hair and the sweeping lines of the face give the portrait movement and energy, as well as describing the texture with great accuracy. Pastel is well-suited to this kind of treatment.

4 *More dark brown has now been introduced in the shadowed areas near the face, while the outer edges of the hair have been lightly blended to produce a softer effect.*

out feeling restricted. For short, curly hair, try a light scribbling motion, using a combination of different marks.

An effective method of drawing fine strands of hair is to use the technique of impressing thin lines into the paper with a sharp metal instrument (*see pages 78–79*). The method requires a little planning ahead to ensure that the lines will be in the right relationship to the rest of the drawing, but the results can make it well worth while.

Boy

The texture of the paper used in this work is at once the major element of its style and the determining factor in the way in which the colored pencils have been handled. The portrait is a subtle color composition where strokes have been used not so much for their own merits, but in order to maintain a systematic deposit of pigment on the paper surface, to produce a soft, almost misty, representation. Base colors were roughed in using pigment blocks. Overall tones were then established by carefully working over the entire drawing. As the portrait was built, so details gradually came into focus, line by line, color by color, pulling highlights forward and pushing shadows back to create the illusion of form without structural lines. Lines do show where they represent the texture of the hair, but otherwise they only carry color to the surface of the paper.

1 *In his initial sketch, the artist positioned the model carefully to make full use of the available natural cross-light. Together with the notes made at the bottom of the sketch he determined the colors that he felt would achieve a delicacy in the treatment of the portrait.*

2 *Some of the main colors were blocked in using pigment sticks, which are ideal for large areas of color.*

3 *Because of the texture of the paper it is easy to remove pigment with a soft kneadable eraser in order to accentuate highlights and blend the pigments without smudging the colors.*

EXPERT TIP
Self-portraits—try them "straight" until you get used to taking an objective view of your own face. Then, for a bit of fun, try sketching yourself in the style of a famous artist you admire.

4 *It can be difficult to blend small areas of color, particularly on a rough surface. Here, the blade of a craft knife was used to scratch and mix the pigment in one movement, at the same time flattening the paper's surface to create a slightly smoother highlight.*

5 *The color in the finished work has been applied in very even, soft layers of strokes, creating subtle mixtures by means of overlaying one color on another. The artist has relied on the texture of the surface to create the almost stippled light effects that add to the delicacy of the interpretation. A green halo of light around the figure forms an almost linear silhouette and serves to draw the figure forward out of the intentionally hazy background. The artist used pigment sticks and crayons in gray, pink, green, dark green, cerulean, apricot, black, and white.*

The dancer

Starting with a photograph of a seated dancer the artist drew a couple of sketches in order to plan and reorganize the structural and color elements of the picture into a more desirable form. Having drawn in the areas of the composition as a pale linear structure by retracing the sketch on a lightbox, he then proceeded to block in the major areas of tone. He started with the background as a basis from which to "fill in" and to which he could relate the colors of the figure. Hatched grids of pink and yellow overlap to create an open, stage-lit background in direct contrast to the heavy purples and black of the dancer's dress. The same color texture is again

picked up in the flesh tones, creating not only a sense of unity in color and style, but offering at the same time a foil to the textured treatment of the hair and dress, and the looser, curved hatching used to depict the feather fan.

1 *Using a photograph of the dancer, the artist worked out a rough color sketch, experimenting with the composition and color on the drawing.*

2 *The drawing was enlarged and traced down, using a lightbox. The background is now worked up with curved strokes of cross-hatching, in pink madder and light yellow (top). The overall impression that results is a beautiful warm, apricot glow (bottom).*

3 *The artist starts to work on the hair, applying deep carmine red and black heavily, but working with the flow of the hair and leaving white areas that he will fill in later with richer and lighter colors. The hair is one of the richest color areas in the composition, so it serves as a good guide to future color decisions. The artist has covered the image with paper so that his hand doesn't dampen the paper or smudge the pigment.*

4 *Using very distinct areas of cross-hatching the artist lays color into the structure of the face. Pale browns form the basis of the grid system, becoming tighter in areas of shadow where blue-violet has also been used to suggest a deeper color.*

5 *Each element of the composition is worked up separately. Here, the flowers in the dancer's hair are left very pale, with touches of gray-green and blue-gray being used to suggest shadows between the petals. Soft yellow tinges the flowers with a warm highlight and echoes the yellow highlight on the hair.*

7 *Reflected color from the background is picked up in the back of the dress with delicate strokes on lilac. The color cast is drawn into the stripes, gradually replacing the black and purple.*

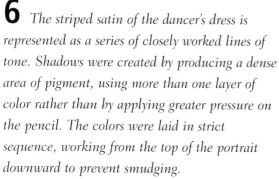

6 *The striped satin of the dancer's dress is represented as a series of closely worked lines of tone. Shadows were created by producing a dense area of pigment, using more than one layer of color rather than by applying greater pressure on the pencil. The colors were laid in strict sequence, working from the top of the portrait downward to prevent smudging.*

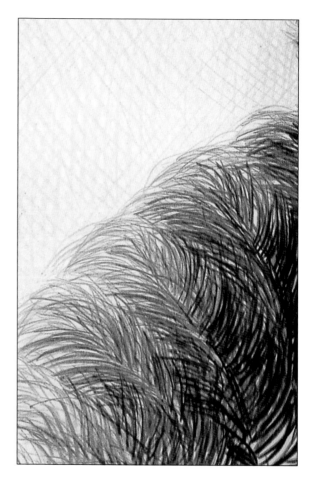

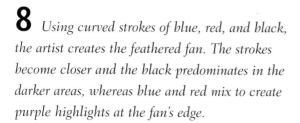

8 *Using curved strokes of blue, red, and black, the artist creates the feathered fan. The strokes become closer and the black predominates in the darker areas, whereas blue and red mix to create purple highlights at the fan's edge.*

9 *The finished drawing is a good example of the complexity of color and the directional qualities of line that may be achieved with hatching and cross-hatching. With very fine linework, the hatching is barely discernible in areas.*

Young woman

The artist chose to portray a close friend of his, because she would be more relaxed while he drew her portrait than a stranger would be. Having traced a very accurate network of guidelines using a lightbox he proceeded to draw in the background with increasingly strong strokes, resulting in a very controlled build-up of pigment. The bottle green color forms a backdrop and acts as a key against which the darkest areas of tone are then drawn. A portion of the model's sweater is colored up to offer a balance for the flesh tones that are then applied in very delicate layers under a magnifying glass. The artist often uses a magnifier so that he can exercise a precise control over his color mixing. Using extremely delicate strokes the skin color is built up over a flat pigmented base—almost a parallel to the way in which the model might apply make-up, working from the lightest tones to the darkest, from the palest to the brightest.

1 *The artist chose a very strongly cross-lit black and white photograph (left) as reference for this work. Using a lightbox, he made a tracing of the image (right) with a brown pencil and will use this as a guideline for the portrait.*

2 *With delicate regular upward strokes of olive green he blocks in the background, taking care at all times to maintain an evenly sharp pencil point. For this an electric pencil sharpener was used.*

3 *Over the olive green the artist places careful layers of bottle green and then dark turquoise, Prussian blue, and Delft blue. Ridges of the olive green are left so that the result is a complex deep color with inherent texture.*

4 *Having firmly established the color of the background, the artist now starts on the head, working almost systematically from top to bottom. Using ultramarine and indigo as an underlayer he colors up the hair. These blues give the later black layers a glow and depth that they would not otherwise have had.*

5 *A pale raw sienna flesh tone is laid as a foundation to the skin areas, leaving highlight areas pale and increasing pressure over the shadowed zones.*

6 *Over the foundation color a deeper brown and pink were used for the areas of tone and shadow. The artist worked from dark to light, building up the deeper colors before deciding how pale to leave the highlights.*

7 *Carefully masking off areas to enable him to see the tones working together, the artist used a magnifying glass to allow him greater accuracy and for drawing in fine details such as the eyelashes, eyes, and edges of the ears. The colors are built up very slowly to create a smooth, matt surface.*

8 *He now uses the nib point of a mapping pen to scratch away thick pigment from the hair color to indicate a highlight sheen. Notice how successfully the blue-green background shines through, not only creating a pleasant depth to the hair color but linking the subject and her surroundings.*

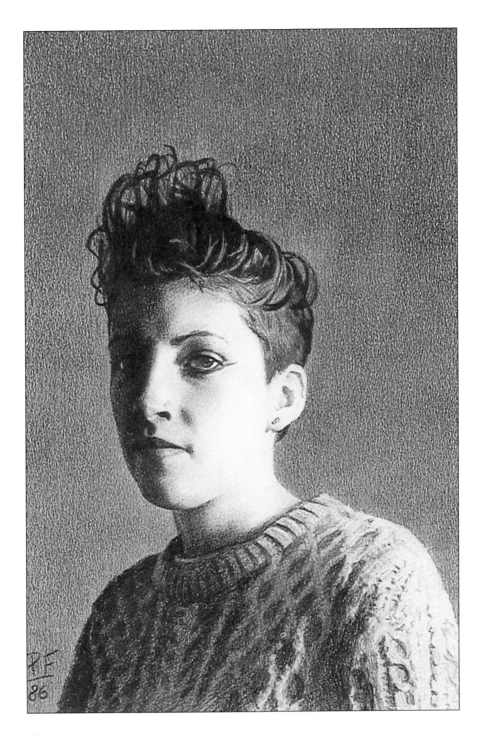

9 *The finished drawing is almost photographic in the rendering. While retaining the same tonal values as the original black and white print the colored version explores many areas of interpretation that are completely lost in the photograph. The background has been worked across the texture of the paper very cleverly, making maximum use of the surface while the more delicate textures in the subject have remained smooth in finish. The layering of color has built up subtleties that a camera would never find.*

Gallery

LIZZIE WITH PLUMED HAT
by Elsie Dinsmore Popkin

The sweeping plumes are described with long directional strokes of the pastel, while on the clothes, skin, and parts of the background the artist has used the feathering technique, in which individual colors are placed over each other without blending.

MARIA
by Gwen Manfrin

The strong contrast of red and black gives this work immediate impact. The artist has kept the internal modeling of the materials to a minimum so that their texture is largely conveyed by their open structure.

BROWNIE GIRL
by Beverly Ferguson Deevy

*Strong side lighting, as used here, can be very
effective in revealing creases and folds in materials.
Using a close range of browns and yellows, the artist
has lovingly described each dip and undulation of the
girl's uniform. Notice also how she has captured the
subtle tones of the folds in the white blouse, where
the shadows are illuminated by reflected light.*

DRAWING ANIMALS

Animals as subject matter for drawing have a longer history than any other subject. The first images drawn by the human race depicted animals that were hunted for survival: the prehistoric cave drawings at Niaux in France, are some of the best preserved examples. Animals are a fascinating subject because, like dancers, they move beautifully and make beautiful shapes. Horses galloping, dogs alert, cats stretching, kittens playing or just laying down and sleeping, are some of the subjects available to us.

Capturing the moment

The drawing of animals presents several pictorial problems unique to the subject matter. Unlike a human, few animals obey a command to remain still. The use of a viewing frame or squared-up paper is thus of little assistance. A good place to start drawing animals is at the zoo. However, even for a skilled artist the constant movement of a tiger pacing an enclosure can present tremendous difficulties. Speed and subtlety of observation are required to draw animals in this environment. Before any attempt is made to put pencil to paper, therefore, observe the animal for some time—how it moves, the size of its head, the proportion and weight of the limbs—and then with the animal in front of you create a drawing that is made as much from your visual memory and imagination as it is from direct representation.

When the beginner first tries to draw animals at the zoo, he or she should try to arrange that the time spent there includes feeding time. This is the one time when, although the animals are no less active, they are more generally in one place.

ELEPHANT

This elephant has been drawn with a fiber-tipped pen that is great for sketches and, since it is very black, it can be used to great dramatic effect.

Most drawing media are suitable; selection really depends on personal choice. The speed at which charcoal can be used with little pressure perhaps has a certain advantage for the beginner.

Photographic reference may also be of some help but should, if possible, be used in conjunction with visual notes made in the presence of the animal that is to be drawn. It does not matter how good or faithful to life the photograph of a tiger might be, there is no substitute for the first-hand experience of seeing the sheer power and size of a fully-grown tiger on the move, even in a zoo enclosure.

If photographs are to be used, it is far better to use photographs that you have taken yourself, for they will act not only as a reminder of the visual appearance of the animal, but they will also remind you of your own feelings toward it.

Every animal has its own character and each of us perceives that character differently, as can be seen in the two very expressive drawings on this page. The better you know an animal, the more there will be to convey in the drawing. You will see signs of age, character, and temperament, that are only visible after time.

MISS EMMA
by Kay Gallwey

CORRIGAN BAN
by K. F. Barker

Elephants

This drawing in black Conté and white chalk was made from original sketches that were drawn at the zoo and also from the artist's memory. Elephants have a marvelous character, are kind and funny animals, and make lovely shapes to draw.

1 *First, the artist simply looked, then started drawing with energy. She put in the main lines, checking the proportion as she drew.*

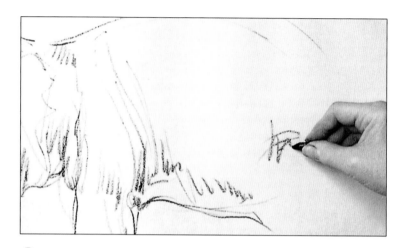

2 *Remember, however big and bulky an elephant looks, the viewer must see the skeleton underneath. Note how long his front legs are and how the belly slopes down to the back legs. The artist has tried to describe how bony the big head is compared with the loose-skinned back legs and rump.*

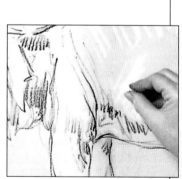

3 *White chalk was used to bring out the shape and describe the rough texture of the skin.*

ELEPHANT IN PASTEL

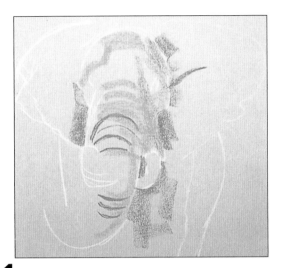

1 *The main form of the head is quickly sketched in with bold side strokes and a limited range of colors.*

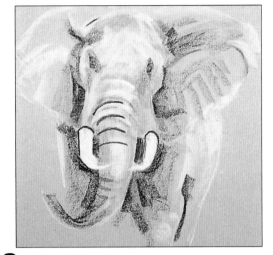

2 *Black pastel behind the head and trunk helps give definition to parts of the drawing as well as bringing the head forward.*

3 *The rough concertina-like skin of the elephant's trunk is built up with layers of short strokes.*

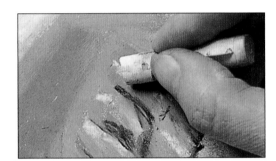

4 *The smoother texture of the ear is created by blending the colors before introducing the small highlights.*

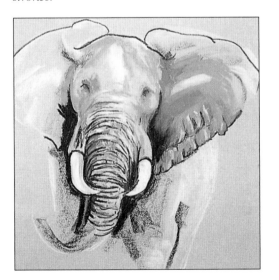

5 *Although the rendering is not complete, the textures have already been suggested convincingly.*

Dog and kitten

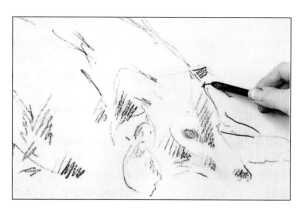

1 *The picture was roughed out lightly, getting the main lines down, going from one part to another again and again, relating each part to another. Drawing imaginary lines with your eyes or putting a ruler across the reference to see what parts are in line with each other is useful. Check the proportions and get the "bones" of the animals in. Remember that they are solid shapes in space, and place them within a background, middle, and foreground.*

2 *Bring in the color and texture.*

4 *When drawing two animals like this, make sure they are relating to each other and that they are both drawn up to the same stage.*

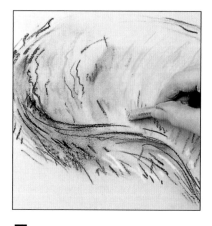

3 *White chalk was used not only for the color of the coat but to highlight and describe form. By now the artist had built up the whole body, and now started to look at detail. The expression and character in the eyes are most important. Black pastel was used on the coat for coloring, but a sharpened black Conté crayon was used to "draw" with.*

5 *Now is the time to adjust any minor mistakes, making sure that the shape of the dog could be seen under his coat.*

6 *In a drawing like this make sure you describe the type of animals portrayed. Stand back frequently to consider the progress of the picture overall.*

7 *Next bring up the texture of the coats. This is all important for animals, as would textures of clothes be if drawing people.*

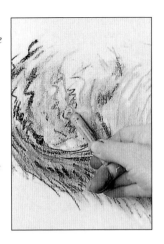

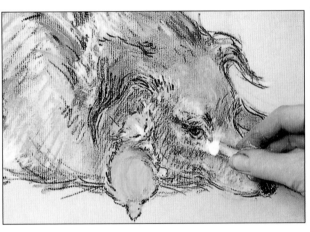

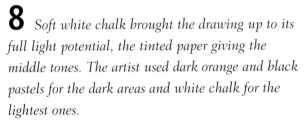

8 *Soft white chalk brought the drawing up to its full light potential, the tinted paper giving the middle tones. The artist used dark orange and black pastels for the dark areas and white chalk for the lightest ones.*

9 *Some shadow was needed to anchor the animals in the picture and give the dog a base to lie on. Here, it was particularly important because she had not drawn any background.*

10 *In the finished drawing you can see a good deal of the tinted paper between the pastel strokes; this adds life to the picture.*

Gallery

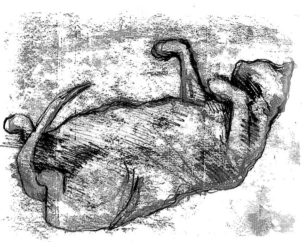

CAT STUDIES
by Judy Martin

These two drawings investigate different ways of describing the form with color. Both examples rely on the contour, first using charcoal and acrylics to describe the massed shape of the body (left), then using a monoprint technique to sketch in overlaid layers of textured color (above).

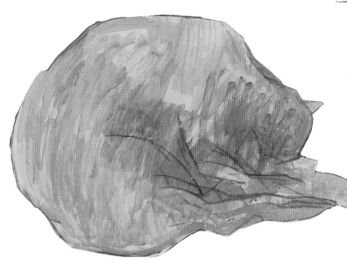

YORKSHIRE TERRIERS
by Daphne Casdagli

This drawing uses heavy strokes of oil pastel to describe the cast shadow of a window frame forming a checkered pattern of light on the floor. The color range is extended by the little dogs playing in the light on the floor, with contrasts of blue-gray where the light falls on their backs against the warm browns and yellows of the fur on their faces and undersides.

USING COLORED PAPER

The color of the paper suggests the
heat of the Middle Eastern setting in
this Conté drawing of a camel.

Glossary

Aquarelle A drawing colored with thin washes of watercolor paint or a painting consisting of overlaid transparent washes.

Aqueous A term that refers to a pigment or medium soluble, or capable of being suspended, in water.

Binder A medium that can be mixed with a powder pigment to maintain the color in a form suitable for painting or drawing. For example, gum is the binder used in making both pastel sticks and watercolor paint.

Blocking in Establishing the main forms and composition of an image with areas of color and tone.

Body color Body color may be used to add highlights, tone or patches of local color in a drawing.

Burnishing Rubbing over a color with an eraser, a paper stump, a tortillon, or even another color, to create a sheen on the underlying color.

Calligraphic A term referring to a linear style of drawing, characterized by flowing, rhythmic marks.

Charcoal A drawing material made by reducing wood, through burning, to charred, black sticks.

Cold-pressed A term applied to high-quality drawing or watercolor paper, referring to its surface, which is medium-smooth. Also known as Not (Not Hot-Pressed).

Complementary colors Those colors that are opposite each other in the color wheel, such as red and green, violet and yellow, orange and blue. Each one increases the intensity of the other when they are juxtaposed.

Composition The arrangement of various elements in a drawing or painting, for example, tone, contour, color, etc.

Conté crayon A drawing stick like a hard, square-sectioned pastel, available in black, white, gray, red, and brown.

Cross-hatching A technique of laying an area of tone by building up a mass of criss-cross strokes, rather than with a method of solid shading.

Earth colors A range of pigments derived from inert metal oxides, for example, ochers, siennas, and umbers.

Figurative This term is used in referring to drawings and paintings in which there is a representational approach to a particular subject, as distinct from abstract art.

Fixative A thin varnish sprayed onto drawings in pencil, charcoal, pastel, or chalk. It forms a protective film on the work to prevent the surface from being blurred or smudged.

Foreshortening The effect of perspective in a single object or figure, in which a form appears considerable altered from its normal proportions as it recedes from the artist's viewpoint.

Gouache A water-based paint made opaque by mixing white with the pigments. Gouache can be used to lay thin washes of color but because of its opacity it is possible to work light colors over dark and apply the paint thickly to emphasize highlights or textural quality.

Grain The texture of a support for painting or drawing.

Masking The use of adhesive tape or masking fluid to protect an area of a drawing while working on another adjacent area.

Medium This term is used in two distinct contexts in art. It may refer to the actual material with which a drawing is executed, for example, pastel or pencil.

It also refers to liquids used to extend or alter the viscosity of paint, such as gum or oil.

Modeling In drawing, modeling is the employment of tone or color to achieve an impression of three-dimensional form by depicting areas of light and shade on an object or figure.

Monochrome A term describing a drawing executed in black, white, and gray only or one color mixed with black and white.

Not A finish in high quality papers that falls between the smooth surface of hot pressed and the heavy texture of rough paper.

Ochers Earth colors in a range from yellow to red-orange, the pigments being derived from oxide of iron.

Optical mixing The juxtaposition in an image of blobs of colors so that they intermingle, but the pigments do not actually mix.

Overhead strokes Strokes applied with a pencil held between the thumb and forefinger.

Pastel A drawing medium made by binding powder pigment with a little gum and rolling the mixture into stick form.

Perspective Systems of representation in drawing that create an impression of depth, solidity, and spatial recession on a flat surface

Picture plane The vertical surface area of a drawing on which the artist plots the composition and arranges pictorial elements that may suggest an illusion of three-dimensional reality and a recession in space.

Pointillism A method of applying color in a series of dots rather than with strokes or in flat areas.

Pouncing A technique of transferring a drawing in which the lines of the drawing are pricked at regular intervals with a pin, and then a sachet of charcoal dust is stamped along the lines.

Primary colors In pigment the primary colors are red, blue, and yellow and cannot be formed by mixtures of any other colors.

Resist This is a method of combining drawing and watercolor painting.

Rough A rough drawing or sketch to be worked up at a later stage.

Sanguine A red chalk used for drawing.

Secondary colors These are the three colors formed by mixing pairs of primary colors; orange (red and yellow), green (yellow and blue), and purple (blue and red).

Sepia A brown pigment originally extracted from cuttlefish, used principally in ink wash drawings.

Sgraffito A technique of incising into the pigmented surface to create texture. Any type of mark can be created using any sharp instrument, from a pin to your fingernail.

Stippling The technique of applying color or tone as a mass of small dots.

Support The term applied to the material that provides the surface on which a drawing is executed.

Tone This is the measure of light and dark as on a scale of gradations between black and white.

Tooth A degree of texture or coarseness in a surface that allows a drawing to adhere to the support.

221

Torchon A stump made of tightly rolled paper, pointed at one end, which is used for spreading or blending a drawing material such as pastel, charcoal, or chalk. It may also be called a tortillon.

Transfer paper Paper coated with a powdery tint used in transferring a drawing from one surface to another.

Underdrawing The initial stages of a drawing in which forms are loosely sketched or blocked in before elaboration with color or washes of tone.

Underhand strokes Strokes made with a pencil held in the palm of the hand and controlled by the thumb and fingers.

Value The character of color or tone assessed on a scale from dark to light.

Viewpoint The angle at which an image is represented to provide the best esthetic study or to emphasize particular elements in the composition.

Index